IMAGES
of America

SOUTHLAKE

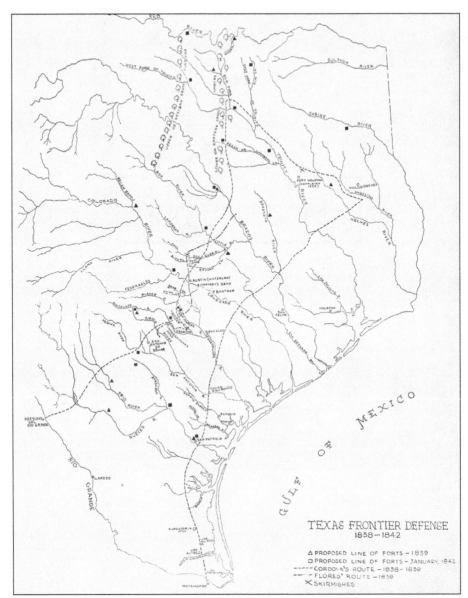

Early cartographers identified the geographic region in which present-day Southlake sits as the Eastern Cross Timbers. The North Texas area was untamed and still a republic when white settlers claimed their land. This 20th-century map was drawn by historian Joseph Milton Nance, one of several maps included in his book. (*After San Jacinto: The Texas-Mexican Frontier, 1836–1841* by Joseph Milton Nance, Copyright © 1963, renewed 1991. Courtesy of the University of Texas Press.)

ON THE COVER: "He had one of the most attractive 80-acre farms that I ever visited in my life," wrote R. E. Smith about his grandfather's property, which included land on both the east and west sides of Carroll Avenue at Continental Boulevard in what is now Southlake. Cantrell Vining Willey moved to the area in 1903 and rented farmland before he purchased this tract of land in the Old Union community, settled by farmers who were members of the Old Union Primitive Baptist Church. (Courtesy of R. E. Smith.)

IMAGES
of America

SOUTHLAKE

Connie Cooley and
The Southlake Historical Society

ARCADIA
PUBLISHING

Published by Arcadia Publishing
Charleston, South Carolina

Library of Congress Control Number: 2009932663

For all general information contact Arcadia Publishing at:
Telephone 843-853-2070
Fax 843-853-0044
E-mail sales@arcadiapublishing.com
For customer service and orders:
Toll-Free 1-888-313-2665

Visit us on the Internet at www.arcadiapublishing.com

Like every Texan boy, Jeroll Shivers grew up wearing cowboy boots. He spent his boyhood in Fort Worth, where he is pictured at age four with his grandfather, J. R. Shivers, and mother, Alno Bailey Shivers. When Jeroll grew up, he moved back to what is now Southlake and picked up where his grandparents left off, farming. This book is dedicated to him.

CONTENTS

Acknowledgments   6

Introduction   7

1.   This Was the West: 1840–1860   9

2.   The Area West of Grapevine: 1860–1900   17

3.   New Generations, Texas-Born: 1900–1920   57

4.   Lessons to Learn: 1920–1935   69

5.   A Rich Past, a Prosperous Future: 1935–1970   97

Bibliography   127

ACKNOWLEDGMENTS

The Southlake Historical Society (SHS) was created in 1992, after resident Gary Fickes placed an ad in the *Grapevine Sun* seeking like-minded people to gather Southlake's history.

Key to this book was information gathered decades ago. In 1979, editor Charles H. Young and other historians, including his wife, Virginia, completed the 548-page *Grapevine Area History*, and a follow-up supplement was published in 1989. We're grateful they included "the area west of Grapevine"—present-day Southlake. Other books, publications, and resources invaluable to the study of Southlake's history are listed at the end of this book.

The SHS has long-standing members, with wonderful recall who helped with this book, including Jack Cook, Lou Hillman, Dr. Bobby Jones, Betty Jones Foreman, Jack Johnson, Wanda and Fred Joyce, Mary Hayes Koenig, Coy Quesenbury, R. E. Smith, Merrill and R. J. Stacy, Wanda Stowe, John R. Tate, Rebecca Utley, Frances Bird Shivers, Crystal and Bob Steele, Aliceanne Wallace, E. I. "Jack" Wiesman, and Charles D. Young. Our dear member Jeroll Shivers has passed on, but the many photographs and memories he contributed made all the difference in this book. Others who contributed information and photographs include former Tarrant County Historical Commission chairwoman Dee Barker and City of Southlake staff members Tara Brooks, Kim Bush, and Patrick Whitham.

To early SHS leaders such as Aloha Payne, Jan Saunders, Zoe Steffanson, Zena Rucker, and others who disassembled an old log cabin, gathered area history, and made a picture inventory of houses that have since been demolished, thank you for caring.

Arcadia Publishing and Hannah Carney, who has been most helpful and patient, deserve our thanks, too.

To Lou Ann Heath, the loyal, faithful, and true SHS member who has seen the group through many changes, thank you. Anita Robeson—whose name should be on the cover of this book as well—is an excellent editor and writer. Thank you, Anita; you are one tireless dog with a bone when it comes to Southlake's history. Finally, thank you to my family. You are the best.

If we have presented something as fact that is not, please accept our apologies. If we have left out pieces of Southlake's history (and we know we have), we sincerely regret it. And, although we've spent sleepless nights thinking about the wonderful photographs of Southlake that are in boxes in someone's attic, we feel the photographs in this book present a full, yet textured, picture of what went on years ago.

—Connie Cooley

INTRODUCTION

It was the land—a blackjack and post oak forest teeming with game, dotted with artesian springs—that enticed people to settle in what today is Southlake.

The Spanish cut their way through it in the 1600s, and theirs were the earliest written descriptions of the Cross Timbers, or what they called *monte grande*—a mix of prairie, savanna, and dense woodland shaped like a dagger that stretched from Central Texas into Kansas. Native Americans had long lived and skirmished with each other here. "It was like struggling through forests of cast iron," wrote author Washington Irving in 1832, after he encountered the forest north of the Red River while traveling.

Republic of Texas president Sam Houston had long sought peaceful approaches to setting boundaries between the increasing number of white settlers and the Native Americans, including the establishment of trading posts such as Coffee's Station, built on the Red River. He also pursued treaties, one of which made the Eastern Cross Timbers the demarcation line between Native Americans and white settlers. In 1843, while waiting for various tribes to arrive for treaty talks, Houston and his entourage camped for one month at Grape Vine Springs, present-day Coppell, where they hunted for buffalo. When the chiefs failed to show up, the meeting was rescheduled; a treaty was eventually signed at Bird's Fort, an early settlement of present-day Arlington.

By the 1860s, there were lots of things around here for settlers to fight—illness, insects, hardship, Comanche Indians, and starting in 1861, the Yankees. Confederate companies were formed in Denton, Dallas, and other towns; and while Northern sentiment prevailed in a few North Texas towns, the men from this area joined the Confederate army and rode east to fight. Many who returned raised families and were buried years later in local cemeteries. Yankees from the North—and even from Southern states such as Tennessee—who came to Texas after the war are buried there, too.

In the economically depressed years after the Civil War, many families and friends trekked to this part of Texas, buying farms carved from the original grants given to the Missouri colonists and establishing scattered churches, schools, and farms. Families made do with what they could grow, and if there was anything left over, a farmer could take it to nearby Grapevine to trade for coffee, sewing needles, or other supplies. Animal pelts also could be traded for supplies.

To get his crops to market in Fort Worth or Dallas, a farmer loaded his wagon and drove to town, arriving late in the evening. He would stable his horses and sleep under the wagon until the market opened early the next day. After selling his crops, he might shop for a few supplies and then head back home.

The Cotton Belt Railroad, running through Grapevine by 1888, expanded markets for his crops. Trucks replaced wagons. If he could afford a truck, a farmer and his sons would only need half a day to deliver their hogs for slaughter in Fort Worth. Tenant farming and sharecropping became more common. R. E. Smith, whose family roots go back to the 1870s in Southlake, described the sharecropper's life in the early 1900s: "Bill Willey was a farmer and worked for [his cousin] Joe on the [Cotton Belt] railroad. Bill's family was referred to as 'sand lappers' because they lived on the sandy land in the Cross Timbers section west of Grapevine, and they were very 'hard scrabble' subsistence farmers." Smith explained that Bill's family would get up early to reach the Grapevine Prairie by dawn, children included. They would "chop" the cotton in the spring, which meant taking a hoe to the rows and weeding and thinning the plants. They'd pick the cotton in the fall and load it in wagons. Smith recalls being thrown into a tall, board-sided wagon full of fluffy cotton and riding in it all the way to the gin in Grapevine.

Area farmers would sometimes have good harvests, but that could mean a larger supply and lower prices. Some negotiated higher prices from processors by joining cooperatives and pooling their harvests. New kinds of farming equipment were replacing the trusted mule- and horse-drawn plows. But despite these improvements, farmers were feeling the pinch of a failing economy by the end of the 1920s. Hardest hit was cotton. In 1932, the price fell from 17¢ a pound to less than 6¢.

The intersection of Highway 114 and Dove Road was the site of the 1934 Easter Sunday shooting of two highway patrol officers by Bonnie and Clyde or members of their gang. E. B. Wheeler and H. D. Murphy had stopped for what they thought were motorists in need of assistance. One of the officers was about to be married, and his bereaved bride-to-be wore her wedding clothes to his funeral. A monument now stands near where they were murdered.

Whether it was the good schools or Southlake's proximity to Dallas–Fort Worth Airport, people liked what they saw when they came to Southlake, and they wanted it to stay that way. Former councilman Ralph Evans called it the "I'm-in-the-boat, pull-up-the-rope mentality." City leaders planned for the future, created master plans that included bike paths and plenty of parks, and held developers accountable for what their city would look like. Whatever the reasons for Southlake's success through good times and bad, the area rich with heritage has endured.

One

THIS WAS THE WEST

1840–1860

When white settlers from Platte County, Missouri, began arriving in the area in the mid-1840s, they established farms, built log homes, and organized the first church in Tarrant County—Lonesome Dove Baptist Church. They were drawn by land promised by the Peters Colony, an *empresario* group that had contracted with the Republic of Texas to recruit settlers.

When empresario contracts expired in 1848, more and more families, most from Southern states, painted "GTT" on their homes, and headed to Texas to try their luck. Some settlers brought slaves. By the mid-1850s, some of the original settlers to the area became disappointed with Texas. "Too crowded," the Reverend John Freeman, the first permanent pastor of the Lonesome Dove Baptist Church, wrote to a friend. A drought discouraged others. So the Reverend Freeman and members of his extended family headed for California. But for a growing number of people, it was here, in this wild, lonely, hardscrabble place, that they found a home.

The dense stands of oak trees in the Cross Timbers separated the Black Prairies on the east from the Grand Prairies on the west. Accounts by Spanish explorer Fray Francisco Caliz, as early as 1718, describe the *monte grande*. "The name fits it," wrote Caliz, "since it is necessary to bring a guide in order to go through it." The needed guides were probably Native Americans familiar with the region. Despite modern-day suburban growth, the scrubby oaks have endured, and remnants of the great forests can be found in Southlake. Intact parcels of the Eastern Cross Timbers, such as this spot photographed in 2004, can be explored in Bob Jones Park and the adjoining U.S. Army Corps of Engineers land in Southlake. (Courtesy of Bob Koontz.)

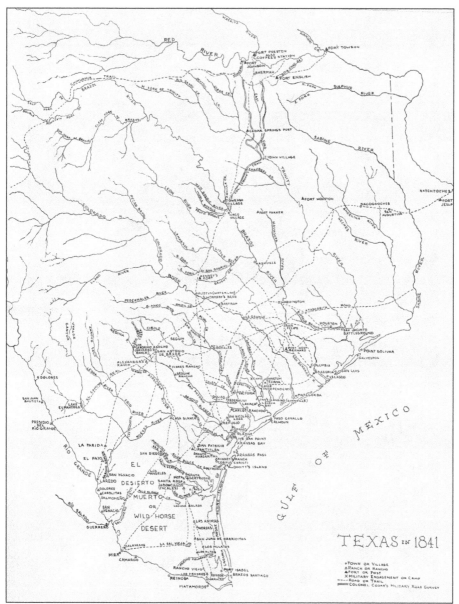

Military forts provided protection for settlers, and this map by Joseph Milton Nance shows the location of the posts in 1841. Private forts were also established by families to protect themselves from Native American raids. Noted on the map is Fort Parker, built near present-day Waco in the spring of 1835 and the site of the most well-known raid in North Texas. On May 19, 1836, Comanches and other tribes attacked the fort. Seventeen settlers fled, but nine-year-old Cynthia Ann Parker and four others were captured. Cynthia Ann was adopted by the tribe and later married a Comanche warrior; one of her sons, Quanah Parker, became an influential Comanche chief. Texas Rangers found her 25 years later during a raid on a Comanche camp, and her uncle, Isaac Parker, took her to Birdville to live with his family. She never readjusted to white society and was never reunited with her Native American family. (*After San Jacinto: The Texas-Mexican Frontier, 1836–1841* by Joseph Milton Nance, © 1963, renewed 1991. Courtesy of the University of Texas Press.)

Malinda Dwight was just 16 when she, her husband, their baby, and 14 other members of the Dwight, Frost, and Parker families fled Fort Parker. Malinda's father and brother were among those who stayed behind to buy time for the others and were killed. The escapees ran to the river bottoms of the Navasota, then trekked five days in uninhabited country before finding safety. After the death some years later of George Dwight, Malinda's husband, she married Allen Hill. In 1870, at age 49, Malinda died and was buried in the oldest cemetery in Tarrant County, the Lonesome Dove Cemetery. Her headstone, pictured here, was carved by one of her sons and has a dove on the back. One of Malinda's descendants, Southlake resident Jack Cook, is the cemetery's longtime caretaker. (Author's photograph.)

The Lonesome Dove Baptist Church was organized in February 1846. While founding members discussed a name for their church, according to Pearl Foster O'Donnell, a dove "perched high in the tree above them [and] began to coo . . . it sounded so lonely and the perfect name for this lonely outpost." The first church was made of logs; pictured is a later structure. (Courtesy of the Tarrant County College District Archives, Fort Worth, Texas.)

Church services took the entire weekend, giving parishioners time to walk to the service; settlers were afraid that if they rode their horses Comanche Indians would steal them. One minister proclaimed what most settlers felt about the raiding Comanches: the first church was built "on a foundation of rocks stained by the blood of an Indian." This picture of church members dates to the 1860s. (Courtesy of the Joyce family.)

13

The Reverend John Allen Freeman, pictured here in his later years, joined the Missouri caravan to Texas as a young man with his wife, Nancy Harris Freeman. They crossed the Red River in 1845. "I was just entering my twenty-fifth year, full of life and full of hope, and an earnest desire to preach Christ in this new and strange land," he wrote. (Courtesy of the Tarrant County College District Archives, Fort Worth, Texas.)

The men and sole woman—she's dressed in white and seated at upper right—of the Lonesome Dove Baptist Church may have gathered for this 1899 photograph while attending the annual church homecoming. Some seen here may have actually been members at sister churches, such as Mount Gilead or Birdville Baptist Church. Note the many bearded men holding canes, most likely veterans of the War Between the States. (Southlake Historical Society collection.)

A number of the charter members of Lonesome Dove Baptist Church and their descendants lie in the historic cemetery adjacent to the church. Members of the Cook family, for example, are buried there. "Lem Cook ran a general store for many years and could be called the first and last Dove banker," according to Frances Higgins Hogue, a longtime Southlake resident. "Everybody farmed for a living and would buy supplies on credit until the crops were harvested. Lem would take a lien against the crops. As the story goes, one farmer died and ended up in Hell. In Hell, a basket was turned upside down. As one of the residents reached down to turn it up, the farmer said, 'Don't turn that basket over! Lem Cook is under there, and he will have a lien on half of Hell.' " Several of the original fieldstone markers of pioneer families remain, and readable headstones date from the 1860s, although the first graves were most likely dug in the 1840s. The Lonesome Dove Cemetery Association maintains the cemetery with private donations. (Author's 1994 photograph.)

A brief history of Lonesome Dove Baptist Church is recorded on this pink granite marker located in front of the church. (Courtesy of E. I. Wiesman.)

LONESOME DOVE BAPTIST CHURCH, CEMETERY

MINUTES PRESERVED 1846 - 1968

ORGANIZED FEB. 1846 IN CHARLES & LUCINDA THROOP HOME

3 MI EAST BY 12 BAPTISTS; JOINED THE NEXT DAY BY

11 BAPTISTS. ELD. J. HODGE, DEACON JAMES GIBSON

FORMED THE PRESBYTERY. 1ST BUILDING AT THIS SITE 1847.

WHEN ELECTED ELD. JOHN FREEMAN, WHO HAD SERVED AS

TEACHER & PART TIME PREACHER SINCE 1846, HE SERVED AS

PERMANANT PASTOR 1847 - 1857. IN ADJOINING CEMETERY

REST MANY TARRANT COUNTY PIONEERS, SEVERAL AMONG 1ST

ELECTED OFFICIALS WHEN IT WAS ORGANIZED IN 1850.

(COPIED FROM HISTORICAL MONUMENT)

CONSTITUENTS

HALL MEDLIN CLERK

JOHN FREEMAN MODERATOR

NANCY (HARRIS) FREEMAN

MARY MEDLIN ANDERSON

SUSANAH (MEDLIN) FOSTER

LUCINDA (FOSTER) THROOP

MARY ANN (FOSTER) LEONARD

FELIX MULLIKIN

RACHEL FOSTER MULLIKIN

HENRY SUGGS

SALETA (FOSTER) SUGGS

HENRY ATKINSON

"THIS COPY PRESENTED AT HOMECOMING, JUNE 11, 1995"

The inscription on the granite is difficult to read. At a 1995 church homecoming, a copy of the inscription was handed out and is shown here. (Courtesy of E. I . Wiesman.)

Two

The Area West
of Grapevine
1860–1900

By the 1860s, families had formed communities here with churches or schools as their meeting places. Most everyone had something in common—they were poor, dirt poor.

Unlike the black dirt on the prairie just miles to the east, the sandy soil in present-day Southlake was hard to farm. "This was the poorest land to try to farm and make a living," explained Southlake resident R. E. Smith. "East of Grapevine, where the airport is today, was the Grapevine Prairie, which was the most productive land in all the state of Texas." Cotton was king on the prairie, but peanuts, corn, and potatoes grew well in sandy soil.

The Dove community grew up first. It began along Dove Road north toward Lonesome Dove Baptist Church. People who lived and farmed as far away as Argyle went to "the Dove" to trade, have their harnesses fixed, or go to church.

The White's Chapel community began in the winter of 1871, when 14 families from Georgia, traveling along a wagon trail that is roughly today's FM 1709, found the area to their liking.

The Old Union community was named for the Old Union Primitive Baptist Church. Its members prayed in a building along Old Union Church Road, which is present-day Continental Boulevard at Brumlow Avenue. The building also served as a school and fraternal lodge.

At the intersection of today's FM 1709 and Davis Boulevard, the Jellico community was a store with a post office, a gristmill, and a sorghum press—all built by one family, the Wilsons.

Over the years, due to economic failure or families moving on, Old Union and Jellico disappeared, but as recently as the 1950s, the *Grapevine Sun* reported the doings in the area west of Grapevine, including the Dove and White's Chapel communities.

Sam Street's 1895 Tarrant County map shows the Dove community on the route between Roanoke and Grapevine. Sam Street's maps were published by the Texas Map Publishing Company in Fort Worth. Customers prepaid for the service, and the maps were mailed to them. The original land grant holders are indicated on the map along with towns and communities, schools, cemeteries,

brickyards, and apple orchards. Other information noted on Sam Street's maps included county voting precincts and the number of votes that were cast as of the most recent election. (Courtesy of E. I. Wiesman.)

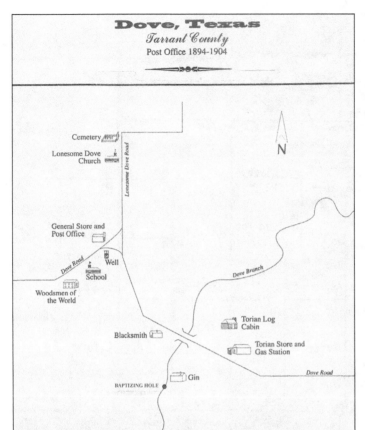

Dove, Texas
Tarrant County
Post Office 1894–1904

Cemetery
Lonesome Dove Church
Lonesome Dove Road
General Store and Post Office
N
Dove Road
Well
School
Woodsmen of the World
Dove Branch
Blacksmith
Torian Log Cabin
Torian Store and Gas Station
Gin
BAPTIZING HOLE
Dove Road

Local historian E. I. "Jack" Wiesman used recollections from longtime residents to recreate the Dove community as it existed from 1894 to 1904. (Courtesy E. I. Wiesman.)

Area farmers came to the Dove general store for provisions. Milk cans lined up on the porch testify to the dairy farming being done here at the beginning of the last century. (Courtesy of the Shivers family.)

The Dove School and general store drew water from the same well, the remains of which are pictured here. Almost every farmhouse had a well. In 1949, Mattie Lowe took pencil and tablet in hand and visited homes, recording family stories: "[Some years ago,] one of the Hogan girls went to draw a bucket of water when the poles that held the pulley fell in and her on top of it. . . . The girl was rescued from the well unhurt." (Courtesy of the Shivers family.)

Woodmen of the World was a men's group organized in 1890 to provide life insurance and other benefits to members. This ribbon belonged to a Torian family member and reads *Dum tacet clamat*, "Though silent, he speaks." Members received distinctive grave markers with the symbols of the fraternal order, including an ax and a stump. Several WOW headstones are found in the Lonesome Dove Cemetery. (Southlake Historical Society collection.)

In 1886, John R. Torian purchased a log cabin "built along a creek at the edge of the Cross Timbers," according to a Texas historical marker. The cabin sat east of Lonesome Dove Baptist Church until 1975, when it was dismantled, and it was rebuilt on Main Street in Grapevine in 1976. (Southlake Historical Society collection.)

Torian family members occupied the cabin until the 1940s. Pictured are, from left to right, William T. "Buck" Sowell (brother-in-law of John Torian; he lived in a log cabin nearby), John Torian, and Ella Torian, John's daughter. Note the fancy bed on the porch. (Southlake Historical Society collection.)

Identified only as a Cate reunion in the Dove community, it's likely that with so many musicians for kinfolk, the family was anticipating some serious toe tapping and, unless everybody there was a Baptist, lots of dancing. (Courtesy of the Tarrant County College District Archives, Fort Worth, Texas.)

Also in the Dove community was the home of Tom and Fannie Cate and their son, Stephen Milton, seen here in a suit and bare feet. Note the barbed wire, which made its way to Texas by the 1870s. (Courtesy of the Tarrant County College District Archives, Fort Worth, Texas.)

Jarrett Foster, seated center, came to Texas as a boy and grew up in the Dove community. He lived in the area for 68 years and was buried in Lonesome Dove Cemetery. His headstone reads: "Last survivor of the first settlers of Missouri Colony and charter member of Lonesome Dove Church, first Baptist church west of the Trinity River." Foster is shown with his five sons in this 1896 photograph. (Courtesy of the Tarrant County College District Archives, Fort Worth, Texas.)

A year after returning from the War Between the States, Spencer Graham married Martha Ann Reynolds. They established a home, shown here, in the Dove community between present-day Peytonville and Randol Mill Roads. (Courtesy of the Shivers family.)

At age 21, Spencer Graham enlisted in the Confederate cavalry and furnished a horse valued at $115, horse equipment worth $12, and a gun valued at $25. He was captured twice. The muster roll of Company G, 18th Texas Cavalry lists Graham and W. O. Medlin, a familiar last name from another early-Texas family. (Courtesy of the Shivers family.)

```
Grapevine, Texas.,                    FEB.11/1913.,
                    * MEMBERS *
         * OF CO.G.THE 18-th TEXAS CAVALRY *
Copy from a list dic't. by Spencer Graham, a member of the
                    above Co.G.
Capt.Felix Mc.Kitrick--Newton Reynolds-----John Malone
Lieu't.Bob Hopkins    Bill Reynolds      Hard Baggin Mc.Aim
Lieu't.Bill Brown     Bill Loving        George Bull
Lieu't.Chas.Robinson  Joe Loving         Perl Farris
Serg't.Jim Eads       Dr.Burnit          Tom West
Serg't.Curtis Kelsey  Tarolton Bull      Ambros West
Serg't.I.R.Burlison   Jack Cook          Noah Myers
Chock Brown           Bryak Mc.Quinn     John Mc.Comes
Thomas Craft          Brack Mc.Quinn     Dave Mc.Comes
I.O.Crawford          Frank Cash         Sol Robards
Indy Crawford         Billy Birdsong     John Akison
Bill Crawford         Wess Long          John C.Cortney
Jess Craft            Edd Long           Old Mr.Stroud
Dave Davis            George Allen       Ash Williams
John C.Castelberry    Onion Head         John Berry
Hugh Mc.Kinsie        Antelope Smith     Acy Pinol
James Medlin          Van Yokley         John Laxton
Dave Mason            George Siegler     John Hucksberry
Frank Wakefield       Jake Siegler       Spencer Graham.
John Gillis           Joe Robinson       --------------
Jim Gillis            Mike Robinson
Adison Gillis         Anthy Robinson
Jack Farris           N.O.Dunham
Marrion Farris        John Martin
Ike George            Sam Martin
Jim Smith             Jim Brown
Bill Lawler           Tom Terry
Bill Paine            John Mc.Caslin
Marrel Paine          John Furgison
Bill Clark            Alex Williams
Jef Terry             John Petty
Sam Haxe              Bill Mc.Kee
Scharly Derrick       Chas. Whitlow
Jeremiah V.           Wisty Fitzhugh
Boon Daugherty        J.O.Hunter
Sam Young             Bill Allen
J.C.Reynolds          John Allen
W.O.Medlin            R.B.Potter
Bob Medlin            M.W.Harris
```

Both Graham and Medlin attended their unit's 40th reunion, held in Dallas in 1902. The surviving soldiers from McKittrick's Company were about 60 years old, but most look older. From left to right are (first row) Capt. R. H. Hopkins, Lt. W. B. Brown, Pvt. A. Williams, and Pvt. Spencer Graham; (second row) Pvt. John Marlin, Pvt. W. O. Medlin, and Pvt. Boone Daugherty. (Courtesy of the Denton Public Library.)

After her husband's death in 1906, Martha Ann Graham, seen here, remained in the Dove community, living with her daughter Bertha. Census records show the Grahams had eight children, five of whom survived their mother. Graham, who lived from 1842 to 1914, is buried in Hood Cemetery in an unmarked grave beside her husband. (Courtesy of the Shivers family.)

SPENCER GRAHAM IS DEAD

ONE OF THE OLDEST SETTLERS OF COUNTY DIED TUESDAY.

Was a Son of a Pioneer and Had Resided in County Since 1854—

Served in 18th Texas Infty.

Spencer Graham, one of the earliest settlers of this county, died at his home in Tarrant county, just over the Denton county line, Tuesday night.

Spencer Graham was about sixty-six years old and was a son of "Uncle" Billy Graham, well known to all of the old settlers of Denton county. He was born in Washington county, Ark., and came to Denton county with his father while a boy. The date of the arrival was about 1854. He at that time joined his father near Argyle, and remained there until the war broke out, when he enlisted in Co. G, 18th Texas, of the Confederate army during February, 1862.

During the early part of the struggle, he was captured at Arkansas Post and carried as a prisoner to Camp Douglass, Ill., where he stayed until he was later exchanged. He then began service in the Tennessee army and served through the remainder of the war. He went through the famous Georgia campaign and on July 22, 1864, was captured at Atlanta and taken to Columbus, O., where he remained until paroled at the close of the war. In February, 1865, he was mustered out and came back to his home here. While in the army Mr. Graham was closely associated with C. A. Williams, W. B. Brown, Boone Daugherty and several other now well known residents of this city and county who went out in the 18th Texas.

In the winter of 1866 Mr. Graham was married to his present wife, who survives him. Several children were born of the marriage, some of whom now make their homes in this county.

Death resulted from a complication of bowel trouble, with which he had suffered for several years, and pneumonia. He had been sick for several weeks.

Interment was made Wednesday at the Medlin cemetery in the southern part of the county.

Spencer Graham's obituary in 1906 details his service in the War Between the States. The newspaper account mistakenly gives his interment at the Medlin Cemetery; he is buried in Hood Cemetery, now part of the Coventry subdivision in present-day Southlake. (Courtesy of the Shivers family.)

This early photograph of Spencer Graham's headstone in Hood Cemetery shows a tall, obelisk-topped marble marker. The inscription simply states: "S. Graham, Born Dec. 14, 1840, Died Mar. 7, 1906." (Courtesy of the Shivers family.)

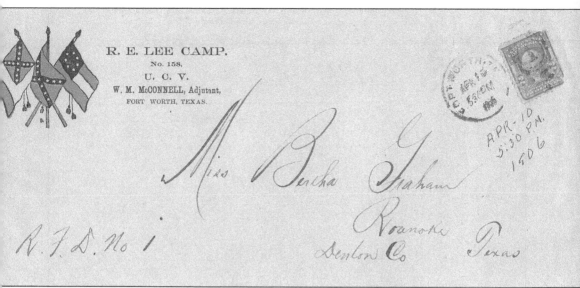

R. E. LEE CAMP.
No. 158,
U. C. V.
W. M. McCONNELL, Adjutant,
FORT WORTH, TEXAS.

Miss Bertha Graham
Roanoke
Denton Co *Texas*

R. F. D. No 1

Upon Graham's death in 1906, the commander of the R. E. Lee Camp, Fort Worth, addressed a letter of condolence, postmarked April 10, 1906, to one of his surviving daughters, Bertha. "R.F.D." in the lower left corner of the envelope stands for "rural free delivery," a service to rural areas established by the U.S. Post Office in 1896. Until then, families traveled to a post office to pick up their mail, or they paid a private delivery service to bring it out. When R.F.D. was first proposed, some opposed the service, including town merchants who feared that their business would suffer because farming families would come to town less often. (Courtesy of the Shivers family.)

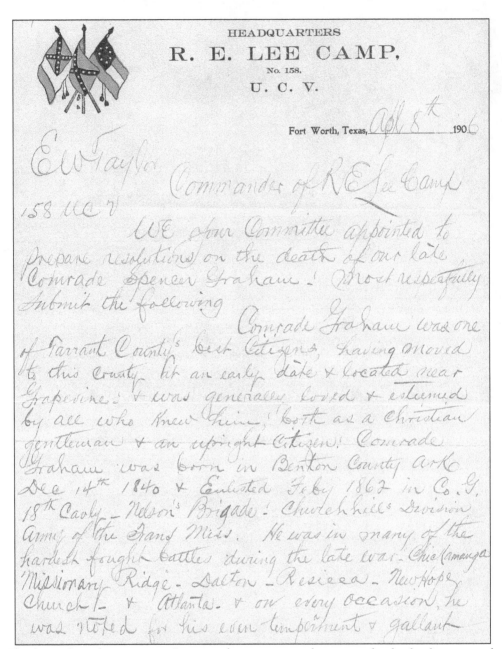

HEADQUARTERS
R. E. LEE CAMP,
No. 158.
U. C. V.

Fort Worth, Texas, Apl 8th 190 6

E W Taylor
Commander of R E Lee Camp
158 UCV

We your Committee appointed to
prepare resolutions on the death of our late
Comrade Spencer Graham! Most respectfully
submit the following

Comrade Graham was one
of Tarrant County's best citizens, having moved
to this county at an early date & located near
Grapevine! & was generally loved & esteemed
by all who knew him, both as a Christian
gentleman & an upright citizen! Comrade
Graham was born in Benton County Ark
Dec 14th 1840 & Enlisted Feby 1862 in Co. G,
18th Cavly — Nelson's Brigade! Churchhills Division
Army of the Trans Miss. He was in many of the
hardest fought battles during the late war. Chickamauga
Missionary Ridge — Dalton — Resieea — New Hope
Church! & Atlanta — & on every occasion, he
was noted for his even temperment & gallant

This letter, from the committee "appointed to prepare resolutions on the death of our comrade Graham," lauded Spencer Graham's citizenship, military service, character, and Christian qualities. The abbreviation U.C.V., shown at the top of the letter, stands for the United Confederate Veterans, organized in 1889 to provide for Confederate soldiers' widows and orphans and to establish homes for disabled and indigent veterans. At one time, membership of the U.C.V. included 160,000 former Confederate soldiers. The men were organized into camps within their state, and veterans would meet for reunions. The U.C.V. was active well into the 1940s, and the SCV—Sons of Confederate Veterans—organized in 1896, continues today as "the oldest hereditary organization for male descendants of Confederate soldiers," according to its Web site. (Courtesy of the Shivers family.)

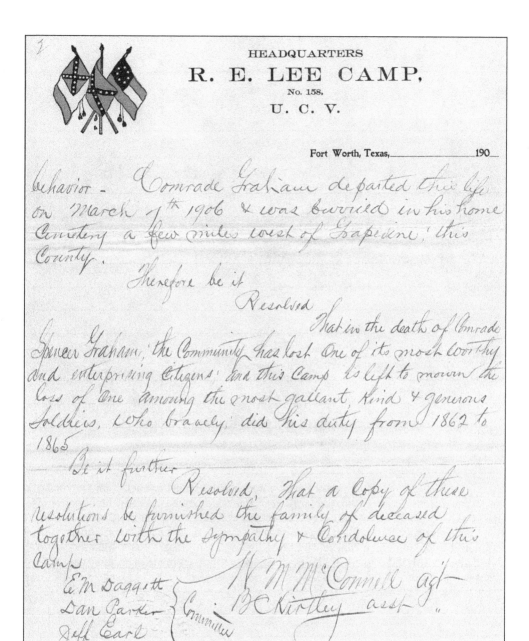

HEADQUARTERS

R. E. LEE CAMP,
No. 158,
U. C. V.

Fort Worth, Texas,_____190__

behavior – Comrade Graham departed this life on March 1st 1906 & was buried in his home Cemetery a few miles west of Grapevine, this County.

Therefore be it

Resolved

That in the death of Comrade Spencer Graham, the Community has lost One of its most worthy and enterprising Citizens And this Camp is left to mourn the loss of One among the most gallant, kind & generous Soldiers, who bravely, did his duty from 1862 to 1865

Be it further

Resolved, That a Copy of these resolutions be furnished the family of deceased together with the sympathy & Condolence of this Camp

E M Daggett
Dan Parker } Committee
Jeff Earl

W M McConnell agt—
B C Kirtley asst "

Approximately 90,000 Texans served in the Civil War, and the tradition of the condolence letter, originally created during the war to advise a family of the dying soldier's last words, continued for decades as a way of offering comfort. In *The Republic of Suffering: Death and the American Civil War*, author Drew Gilpin Faust writes that obituaries often included, word for word, the deceased person's qualities as mentioned in a family's condolence letter (when it sent word of a loved one's death). The detailed descriptions of the soldier's character and Christian qualities seem exaggerated and flowery to today's reader, but Faust insists that condolence letters helped surviving family members "make sense out of a slaughter that was almost unbearable" and helped to soothe the "spiritual wounds" that the war had inflicted upon them. The beauty of the handwriting would make any English teacher swoon. (Courtesy of the Shivers family.)

Bertha and Ora Graham, daughters of Spencer and Martha Ann Graham, were two attractive young women from the area at the beginning of the 20th century. Dressed here like twins—Bertha on the left and Ora on the right—they were two years apart. The style of their clothing, termed belle epoque or Edwardian, was in vogue for women of their day and consisted of an uncomfortable-looking collar that reached right under the chin and was designed to elongate the neck. It certainly did that. Only Ora married, but both sisters made their homes in the Dove community. (Courtesy of the Shivers family.)

John Calvin Graham, at right, and George Bruno Graham, below, were the younger brothers of Ora and Bertha Graham and the last of eight children born to Spencer and Martha Ann Graham. Both blacksmiths, they operated a shop in Dove and lived their lives in the community. The bachelor brothers, dressed fashionably in these photographs, might have been considered candidates for any "most eligible bachelor" list. Their suit jackets and ties look interestingly modern and could probably be worn today to the right occasion. (Courtesy of the Shivers family.)

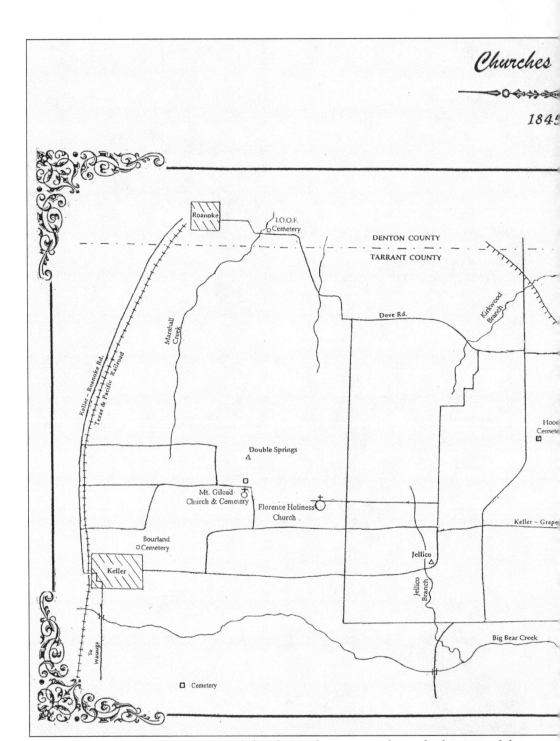

This Northeast Tarrant County map of churches and cemeteries shows the location of the early settlements, their burial grounds, and the rural schools that served them, notably Dove, White's Chapel, Old Union, Sams, and Lone Elm. From 1884 into the 20th century, Texas made important advances to improve public education for rural students. In 1917, three "one-roomers" were consolidated into Common School District No. 99, and in 1919, Carroll School (also known

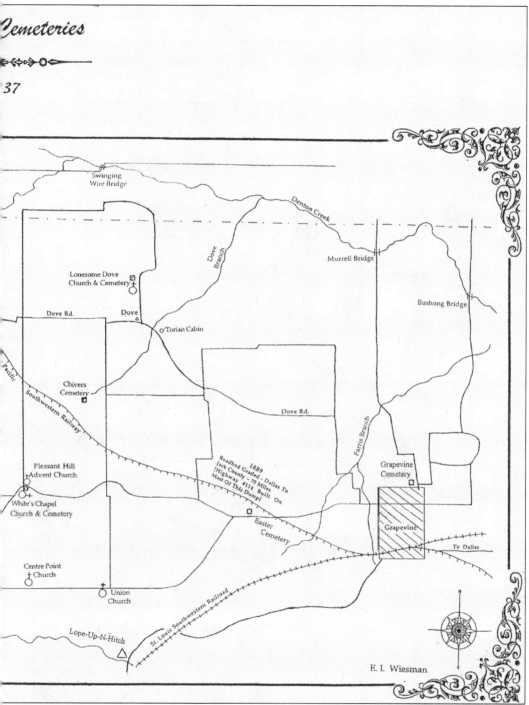

Swinging
Wire Bridge

Denton Creek

Murrell Bridge

Dove
Branch

Lonesome Dove
Church & Cemetery

Bushong Bridge

Dove Rd.   Dove

O'Torian Cabin

Pacific

Southwestern Railway

Chivers
Cemetery

Dove Rd.

Farris Branch

Pleasant Hill
Advent Church

Roadbed 1889
Graded - Dallas To
Jack County - 70 Miles
(Highway #114 Built On
Most Of This Dump)

Grapevine
Cemetery

White's Chapel
Church & Cemetery

Easter
Cemetery

Grapevine

Centre Point
Church

To Dallas

Union
Church

St. Louis Southwestern Railroad

Lope-Up-N-Hitch

E. I. Wiesman

as Carroll Hill School) was built along a wagon road now known as Carroll Avenue. Highway 114 began as a proposed railroad from Grapevine to Graham, Texas. The Dallas, Pacific, and Southwestern Railway went broke, but not before the initial railway bed, or dump, was laid. That dump would later form the groundwork for the highway. (Courtesy of E. I. Wiesman.)

Benjamin M. Wilkinson first journeyed to Texas in 1867 but was forced to return to Georgia to handle his father's estate. Thirty-two years later, Wilkinson, his wife, Nancy Austin Wilkinson, and their children settled in the White's Chapel community to be near her parents, Mary Ann and Stephen Blevins Austin, who led the community's first settlers to the area in 1870. (Courtesy of the Tarrant County College District Archives, Fort Worth, Texas.)

Sarah Wilkinson Castleberry, the daughter of Benjamin and Nancy Austin Wilkinson, was born in Tarrant County before her family returned to Georgia. This picture shows Sarah all grown up with her husband, Uriah Castleberry, seated at left. Years later, their daughter Faithie Jane married into the Jimeson family, which owned property on what is now Shady Oaks Drive when it was called Jimeson-Fowler Road. (Courtesy of the Tarrant County College District Archives, Fort Worth, Texas.)

These quarter-notched, hand-hewn logs are from a single-pen (one-room) log cabin reportedly built around 1865 and inhabited as late as the 1940s. It originally stood south of FM 1709 and east of Carroll Avenue. (Courtesy of E. I. Wiesman.)

In the 1990s, members of the Southlake Historical Society dismantled and stored the logs until a reproduction could be built. These simple cabins would do until a family could build something more substantial. (Southlake Historical Society collection.)

In 2006, the Southlake Historical Society donated logs from three log structures to the City of Southlake, which hired Bill Marquis of Parker County to reconstruct a log house. In a log house, the logs are hewn. A tool called a hand adze—or possibly, a falling or felling ax and a broad ax—is used to make each side flat. The floor is wooden. The notching is half-dovetail, which is a higher quality of craftsmanship. The log house has windows, although not of glass, as that material was hard to obtain. The completed Southlake Log House sits next to Bunker Hill in Bicentennial Park on what was known as Blossom Prairie, a meadow with abundant springs and firewood; it was an early campground for settlers on their way west. (Author's photograph.)

Rebecca Alexander and Louis Napoleon (L. N.) Bailey were married in the early 1900s and had five children. They lived in the White's Chapel community. One of their daughters, Alno Bailey, spoke of the family home place. "I was borned on the hill, up west of White's Chapel, on Grapevine Highway [FM 1709] in 1909," Bailey recalled. Rebecca Bailey died when Alno was two years old. L. N. Bailey remarried within a few years. (Courtesy of the Shivers family.)

The Baileys' house was built in the late 1800s and was said to be the first board house in the community. The structure was one of several that sat on the family's 200-acre farm, which extended south from FM 1709 to present-day Continental Boulevard, between Peytonville Avenue and White Chapel Boulevard. Seen in this 1914 photograph is Louis Napoleon Bailey Jr. (Courtesy of the Shivers family.)

By the 1890s, White's Chapel School had two rooms, one made of logs and the other wood-framed. The school had no well from which to draw water, so the teachers and students got water from a water tank west of the church. But first, a longtime resident recalled, the "cows had to be driven away. Not a great deal of thought was given to germs at the time." (Courtesy of the Shivers family.)

These White's Chapel School students may have been celebrating Easter—a small basket and several toy rabbits holding eggs are lined up in front of them. Notice the barren ground and few trees; settlers cleared the forests of the Cross Timbers to build their houses and to farm. (Courtesy of the Shivers family.)

Stephen Blevins Austin's family was one of the original ones in the White's Chapel area, and the families held church services in his log cabin before building a small log church on land he donated. First named Oak Hill Methodist Church, it was renamed White's Chapel Methodist Church for a popular early preacher. The structure shown here was built in the 1920s to replace others destroyed by wind or fire and has been restored as a chapel. (Courtesy of E. I. Wiesman.)

The first grave inside White's Chapel Cemetery, located at the corner of White Chapel Boulevard and FM 1709, is said to have been a child's, the daughter of a family in a passing wagon train, in 1851. Many of the community's pioneers are buried in the cemetery. White's Chapel Cemetery Association maintains the grounds with private donations. (Author's photograph.)

This farm, located in the Old Union community, was worked by members of three families—the Blevinses, Webbs, and Willeys—whose members gathered in 1910 for this picture. Shown along the fence are, from left to right, Henry Webb, George Webb, Sarah Hardin, Otis Blevins, Ben Blevins, Eula Willey Blevins, Emily Hardin, Sarah Elizabeth Blevins, Nancy Webb, and Taylor Blevins. Sitting on the porch are, from left to right, Annie Isadora Willey Smith and Gladys Zealot Willey. (Courtesy of R. E. Smith.)

Eula and Ben Blevins were married in the large Old Union community farmhouse where he was born, and they worked alongside other family members on the 80-acre farm. The work stopped for no one—Eula is pregnant here with the couple's third child. Their companion dog is close by. (Courtesy of R. E. Smith.)

The original Old Union School was one room and was built in the late 1890s. Members of Old Union Primitive Baptist Church held services there, and so did the Independent Order of Oddfellows (IOOF). The building burned in 1910. Henry Webb remembered as a child looking through rubble after the fire and finding black and white marbles that lodge members used in their voting. (Courtesy of R. E. Smith.)

According to R. E. Smith, grandson of Cantrell Vining Willey of the Old Union community, "As long as a child could read, as long as they could count, that was all the education they needed according to most old-time Primitive Baptists." Several of the Old Union students in this picture, dated 1912, look old enough to have mastered more than the basics. (Courtesy of R. E. Smith.)

Farming the land required dependable work animals and farm equipment and lots of muscle. This interesting piece of equipment drawn by mules was possibly used to cut the hay. Two of the men are holding what could be pitchforks, so gathering it up was most likely left to them. From left to right are unidentified, Ara Dual Smith, unidentified, Dura Alladin Smith, and Arlie (last name unknown). (Courtesy of R. E. Smith.)

This beautiful photograph near the Old Union community captures the early-American spirit of the farmer. The strong draft animals hitched up here are ready and waiting for the signal to get back to work. (Courtesy of R. E. Smith.)

James J. and Miranda Grandberry Joyce moved from Mississippi to Texas in 1852 with their children, grandmother, a slave named Charlotte, and Charlotte's son, Dan. Charlotte, freed after the War Between the States, moved to Collin County and died at age 100. Dan grew up with the Joyce children and is buried in the family plot in Mount Gilead Cemetery. (Courtesy of the Joyce family.)

The Bible that Miranda Grandberry Joyce holds most likely made the trip to Texas with the family. Often a Bible was the only book a family owned, and it contained the records of births, marriages, and deaths. (Courtesy of the Joyce family.)

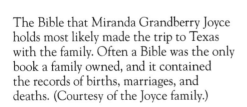

Gen'l Land Office
Austin Jany 25 1860

James Joyce Esq
Grape Vine Texas.

Dear Sir,

Acknowledging receipt of your letter of the 8th instant, I herewith hand you Patent No 943 Vol 17 3rd class for 320 acres issued to John Greenberry assignee of W D Beall

Fee $21.00 charged to acct of your deposit. The above amount exhausts your deposit.

Yours respectfully

Robt M Elgin

Clerk

The General Land Office of the Republic of Texas was established in 1836. Grants issued by other countries, primarily Spain and Mexico, were honored, and all new grants issued by the republic were surveyed and established through the land office. Many headright grants were dependent upon factors such as when the head of the family arrived in the republic; whether he was white, African American, or Native American; and whether he was married. Early on, the republic also contracted with groups that brought settlers into Texas in exchange for land. This letter, dated 1860, indicates that James Joyce was granted a land patent for 320 acres. (Courtesy of the Joyce family.)

The State of Texas, } Know all Men by these Presents:
COUNTY OF TARRANT.

THAT *Mr James Joyce Lucinda Davis and Charles N. Neace*

of the County of *Tarrant* and State aforesaid, in consideration of the sum of

one ($1) DOLLARS

to *us* paid by *the Deacons of the Baptist Church of Christ at Mt Gilead*

of the County of *Tarrant* and State of *Texas* the

receipt whereof is hereby acknowledged, have Granted, Bargained, Sold and Released, and by these

Presents do Grant, Bargain, Sell and Release, unto the said *Deacons and their successors in office forever a certain Parcel of Land as a Burial ground to be known as the Mt Gilead Graveyard. Containing (2 3650/5645 acres less a Reserve Made by James Joyce hereinafter described Situated in Tarrant county Texas on the waters of Bear Creek and More particularly described by being a part of the Daniel Barcroft Survey, Beginning 950 Varas North of the S.E. Corner of the said Barcroft Survey at E.A. Hills N.E. corner, thence North 180 Varas to a Rock, thence West 83 Varas to a Rock, thence S 180 Varas to a Rock in E.A. Hills North line, thence East 83 Varas to the place of Beginning containing (2 3650/5645 acres, less the James Joyce Reserve (to wit) Beginning at the N.W. Corner of the said Mt Gilead Graveyard thence North 96½ Varas, thence West 35¾ Varas, thence North 17¾ Varas, thence North West 13 Varas, thence South 19½ Varas, thence East 12¾ Varas to the place of Beginning of said Joyce Reserve*

James Joyce served as deacon and clerk of Lonesome Dove Baptist Church. In 1852, a sister church was organized, the Mount Gilead Baptist Church in present-day Keller. Two acres were sold to the church for $1 "as a Burial ground to be known as the Mount Gilead Graveyard." According to this 1881 warranty deed, a portion of the land came from the "James Joyce Reserve." (Courtesy of the Joyce family.)

48

The Joyce children attended nearby Sams School, established in the late 1870s on land donated by Calvin A. and Lucinda Sams. Sams School was located in the general area of Dove Road and Sams School Road in present-day Southlake. This picture is dated 1895. (Courtesy of the Joyce family.)

In an oral history given by longtime Dove community resident Claude Lee Shivers, he mentions that his mother taught at Sams School. "They didn't pay very much for school teaching then," Shivers explained. "We found some vouchers in her trunk where she was getting $25 a month." One of the vouchers, dated 1879, is pictured here. (Courtesy of the Shivers family.)

This lively bunch of Sams School students is pictured outside the building in 1916. Boys far outnumber girls, who were often expected to quit school earlier than boys to tend to younger siblings at home. (Courtesy of the Shivers family.)

Sams School students are shown here in 1916. Starting in 1884, even community schools such as Sams were given a number and included in the county school reports. In 1917, Sams was combined with White's Chapel and Dove Schools to form Common School District No. 99. In 1919, when a new brick school was built, Sams School was assessed as being in "bad" condition and was closed and sold. (Courtesy of the Shivers family.)

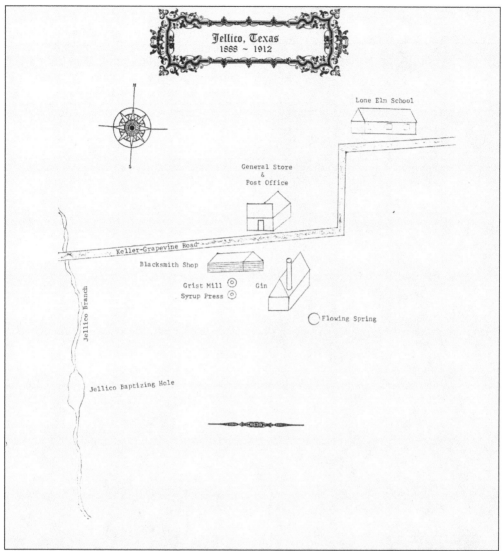

According to the Texas State Historical Commission and local historians, the Jellico community was established in 1881, when Robert Emmett Wilson purchased property on the north and south sides of Keller-Grapevine Road, which is now Davis Boulevard at FM 1709. Wilson later built a general store, and by 1898, a post office had been established. The town was named after the Jellico Ranch, on which the general store was located, so named for Jellico, Tennessee, from which early settlers had originated. This map is an interpretation of the community as it was between 1888 and 1912. (Courtesy of E. I. Wiesman.)

The heavily traveled Jellico-Bransford Road ran south from Jellico to Bransford, an early settlement of present-day Colleyville. As shown in this 1996 picture, the trail is still rutted with rocks worn down by wagon wheels. (Courtesy of E. I. Wiesman.)

Another picture, taken in 1979, shows what local historians call the upper trail of the Jellico-Bransford Road, still wallowed out from heavy wagon traffic. (Courtesy of the Charles H. Young family.)

Robert Emmett Wilson was born in 1845 in Mississippi and moved with his wife, Sarah McGinnis Wilson, to Texas around 1880. Wilson and his family lived in Fort Worth, where he ran a livery stable. According to family records, Sarah's mother "undoubtedly helped" the couple by loaning them the money to purchase their farm in the Jellico community. "They could have bought prairie land for $9 per acre, but wanted a place where there was shallow water and timber, so they paid $11 per acre . . . and moved into an old log house," family records show. (Courtesy of the Shivers family.)

The Wilson log house was located east of present-day Davis Boulevard. Over the years, the structure was altered, including the addition of wood siding as shown in this undated photograph. (Courtesy of E. I. Wiesman.)

The youngest child of the Wilsons, Mary Maude, was born in the house and continued to live there after she married William Henry Brown in 1905. The house was enlarged to accommodate their growing family. This photograph is dated 1990. (Courtesy of the Historic Preservation Council for Tarrant County, Texas.)

Lone Elm School dates from 1877, before Jellico was established. This picture of 19 students, many of them siblings, and their teacher was taken in 1908, just as the price of cotton and cattle began to drop. The resulting hard times were devastating for the community and the Wilsons. Having cosigned on a number of outstanding debts, Robert Wilson was forced to sell the cotton gin and gristmill to cover them. (Courtesy of E. I. Wiesman.)

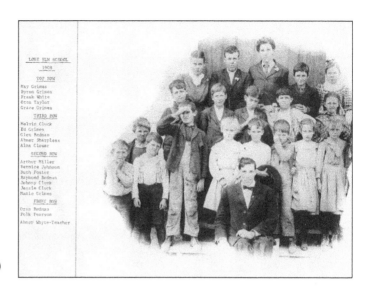

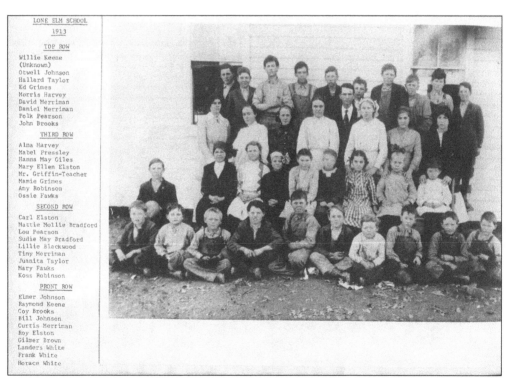

Seated in the front row, sixth from the left, is one of Robert Wilson's grandsons, Robert Gilmer Brown, born in 1907. Brown remembered the community's old general store, and when he was older he told of how the building was cut in two, and "half of it was moved up the hill" near their house to be used as a feed and tack room. (Courtesy of E. I. Wiesman.)

In early years, some students on the west side of present-day Southlake attended Florence School. That school became part of Common School District No. 100, and today a school named Florence is part of the Keller Independent School District. This photograph, dated 1938, shows Boys Scouts of America Troop No. 123, which was attached to Florence School. (Courtesy of E. I. Wiesman.)

The Jellico branch of Big Bear Creek, which runs from Keller through modern Southlake, was a popular baptizing hole. Family members and neighbors in this 1920s picture have lined up along the creek, dressed in their Sunday best and ready to begin. (Courtesy of the Shivers family.)

Three

New Generations, Texas-Born
1900–1920

Into the 1900s, new generations in the area west of Grapevine continued to produce cotton, corn, and grain and raise livestock in much the way their parents had.

For women, housework included endless cooking, canning, floor scrubbing, baby tending, and more. Most families had a milk cow, chickens, and hogs; everyone had a big garden.

During World War I, young men left to fight in France. Spanish influenza, which killed millions worldwide, struck here, too. "They was burying people every day," remembers resident Claude Shivers, who was born in 1907. On Decoration Day, families would tidy up cemeteries.

Will and Bob Lipscomb, brothers who lived in Grapevine, were the area's doctors. "They'd have to come out here either in a buggy or riding a horse," Shivers recalled. "Out in the country, that was the only way to travel. They didn't have any roads, except just old dirt roads, and when it was muddy, why, it was muddy."

In the summer, religious revivals were held in brush arbors—poles with leafy branches spread over the top. Women's groups organized quilting parties and Bible studies, and families enjoyed recreational sports such as community baseball and softball teams.

On Saturday nights, downtown Grapevine was the place to be. "The town would be full of people—of country folks coming to town, and city folks getting together and talking, telling jokes and having a good time," remembered one area farmer.

Telephone service reached White's Chapel and other area communities in the early 1900s, but for many, the best way to communicate was with the dinner bell. "If you heard a dinner bell, up there on a post, a'ringin' any time besides, say 11:30 to noon, somebody needed help," Shivers recalled. "Back then, people helped each other."

By the 1900s, the Cotton Belt Railroad running through Grapevine had expanded markets for farmers' crops. The Cotton Belt line can be dated to 1877, when the Tyler Tap Railroad Company began service between Tyler and Big Sandy in East Texas. By 1891, after many ownership and railway name changes, the Cotton Belt was part of the St. Louis Southwestern Railway Company. The Cotton Belt main line ran west from St. Louis and Memphis through Texarkana to Dallas, Fort Worth, and Gatesville. This lonely Cotton Belt caboose was photographed in 1994 on someone's property near the intersection of Lonesome Dove and Dove Roads. (Courtesy of John Cooley Jr.)

When Ora Graham and J. R. Shivers applied for their marriage license in 1902, Tarrant County was one of several fast-growing counties in the state—from 1890 to 1900, one thousand new farms were reported. Before marriage, Ora had taught at Sams School, but her teaching contract required her to remain single. Instead, she chose to farm alongside her husband and raise a family. (Courtesy of the Shivers family.)

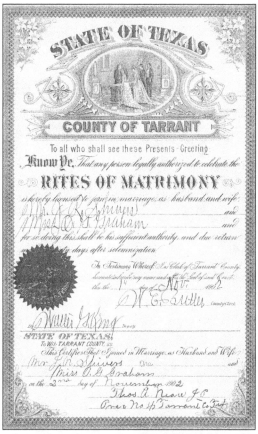

Farm animals were essential. Mules and horses worked in the fields and transported a family to and from school and church. A large portion of the J. R. Shivers family's acreage in modern Southlake was unfenced and used for grazing cattle and hogs and raising cotton, corn, and peanuts. According to family accounts, Shivers's hogs rooted up and ate the peanuts, which fattened them before they were slaughtered. (Courtesy of the Shivers family.)

Farm animals were put to work in handy ways—these goats cleaned out the Shiverses' pasture. This was especially true in the Cross Timbers, where goats were used to destroy small shrubs so that more grass would grow. (Courtesy of the Shivers family.)

J. R. Shivers, seen here with his team of working mules, was one of three trustees of Common School District No. 99 when it was formed in 1917. His name and those of E. E. Higgins and B. F. E. Griffin are engraved in the cornerstone of the original schoolhouse, built in 1919, which still stands. (Courtesy of the Shivers family.)

Farming families depended on themselves for almost everything. In rural areas, mothers bore the burden of tending to sick children and husbands with whatever was at hand. Childhood accidents were frequent, and doctors had to travel miles on horseback to treat the sick. The baby seen on the left in this Tanner family picture would drown in the Dove Branch. (Southlake Historical Society collection.)

Farming children worked hard, and everyone pitched in. Seen here from left to right are Ella, Felix, and James Torian, the children of John R. Torian, who grew up working on the family farm in the Dove community. They also helped run the family-owned general store. (Southlake Historical Society collection.)

Felix "Man" Torian helped with the 360-acre family farm in the Dove community until the 1930s, when he moved to Grapevine and ran a service station. "City life was not for Man Torian," his nephew wrote. "In less then three years, he moved his station 3-1/2 miles northwest of Grapevine on Highway 114 [to present-day Southlake]." Torian ran the station until his death in 1945. (Southlake Historical Society collection.)

Women never ran out of work. "We washed with a rubboard and a pot that we boiled our clothes in," explained Lizzie Higgins. "And when you got through washing, you'd take all of that good, hot soapsuds and go in the house and scrub all the floors." Though looking elegant in this picture, when Mary Elizabeth Hemphill married Felix Torian, she'd grown up used to such work. (Southlake Historical Society collection.)

Eleven months after giving birth to Leona, her only daughter, Mary Hemphill Torian died of typhoid fever. Leona was raised by her maternal grandmother, while her three brothers and father lived in the Torian log cabin. Granny Hemphill is seen here in her later years next to her brother, Civil War veteran and bachelor William "Buck" Sowell, outside the cabin in which Leona was raised. (Southlake Historical Society collection.)

This photograph of sisters Ora Graham Shivers, left, and Bertha Graham, right, was taken at the Hippodrome Postal Studio, 1108-B Main Street, Fort Worth, around 1912. Some farming families had a little extra cash, allowing for a few small luxuries and the occasional outing. (Courtesy of the Shivers family.)

Also enjoying an outing to Fort Worth were Ora and J. R. Shivers's two sons, Cloyce (left) and Claude (right). The boys were raised on the family farm and attended Sams School and Dove School. (Courtesy of the Shivers family.)

It was not all work and no play for the Graham brothers, who were blacksmiths. John Graham, at left, was a musician. (The man on the right is unidentified.) Brother Bruno worked with wood to create baseball bats. Lizzie Higgins recalled, "He'd make those bats for us girls to play ball, and they'd be a wide plank . . . trimmed down for us where we could handle them with our hands. And then he'd draw all pretty drawings on this bat. And they were beautiful bats as well to play ball with. I see them bats in my mind." (Courtesy of the Shivers family.)

"The entire country mounted World War I as a great crusade," wrote Theodore Reed Fehrenbach in his book *Lone Star: A History of Texas and the Texans*. Almost 200,000 Texans saw service in the war. This picture of J. E. Douglass Jr. captures the patriotic fever Fehrenbach wrote about. Douglass and his wife, Oma Blevins Douglass, were longtime residents of the Southlake area and were buried in White's Chapel Cemetery. (Courtesy of R. E. Smith.)

Two infantry divisions of World War I—the 36th and the 90th—were mostly Texans. Both divisions were called T-Patchers because the T-O insignia they wore stood for Texas-Oklahoma, but several sources referred to the troops as the "Tough 'Ombres." James Elie Torian was killed in the war, and his casket is seen here with a military color guard outside Lonesome Dove Baptist Church in 1918. (Southlake Historical Society collection.)

Despite the loss of life fighting overseas, more deaths were related to the 1918 Spanish influenza epidemic. Soon after attending the funeral of his cousin James, Walter Torian (seen next to his uniformed brother, Clint, and their younger sister, Leona, standing outside of the Torian cabin) contracted the flu and died. Other contagious diseases of the day included yellow fever, small pox, measles, and cholera. (Southlake Historical Society collection.)

This photograph shows several Torian generations and speaks to the changing times. The younger women are, predictably, more stylish than the older women. The men, several in straw hats, look more like merchants than farmers. (Southlake Historical Society collection.)

As far back in Texas politics as the 1868 state constitutional convention, legislators had argued for and against a woman's right to vote. Many feared that if given the right to vote, women would neglect their husbands and children and become more like men, leading to the breakdown of the family. But in 1918, Texas governor William Hobby signed into law a woman's right to vote in state primary elections (additional voting rights were given to women in 1920, when a U.S. constitutional amendment was passed). Due in large part to the 386,000 women who registered to vote that same year, the first woman was elected to state office; Annie Blanton, a faculty member at the North Texas State Normal College, now the University of North Texas in Denton, was elected as state superintendent of public instruction. Rural women like Minnie Arterburn Torian, standing with her husband, Clint, would benefit from the political and social changes for women ushered in by the vote. (Southlake Historical Society collection.)

Four

LESSONS TO LEARN
1920–1935

By the early 1900s, Texas legislators began taking education seriously. Goals were made to give uniformity to the curriculum, strengthen teacher training, improve school facilities and equipment, and divide students into separate classrooms. In 1917, White's Chapel, Sams, and Dove Schools were consolidated into Common School District No. 99, and in 1919, it followed the lead of dozens of county school districts in Tarrant County and built a brick school.

Plain, three-room Carroll School (also called Carroll Hill School) opened with 97 students, grades one through nine, one principal who also taught, and two teachers. Built on a hill, the school had plenty of windows to let in light and breezes. Students walked, rode mules, or drove buggies over dirt roads to get there. Its namesake was the Tarrant County superintendent of public instruction, Burrell Estelle Carroll, a popular educator who had taught in Birdville, Hurst, and other neighboring areas.

African Americans living in the area were mostly farmers and laborers. Instead of attending Dove, White's Chapel, or Sams Schools, their children went farther away to what were called "colored schools." Bob Jones was born a slave in 1850, and in the early 1900s, he built Walnut Grove School near the Tarrant-Denton county line for his children and hired a teacher; before that, his family sometimes lived in Denton so the children could attend school. When Walnut Grove School closed in the 1950s, its graduates—including some of his grandchildren—went on to a segregated high school in Fort Worth.

The 1920s brought a measure of prosperity to the area. Farmers had good harvests, but bigger crops often meant lower prices. In the Great Depression that followed, times were tough, and outlaws such as Bonnie and Clyde roamed the area. On Easter Sunday 1934, the gang shot dead state troopers H. D. Murphy and E. B. Wheeler. A local man now in his 90s recalls seeing a lone Ford sedan sitting at the top of the hill on Dove Road that morning, but when he and his pals passed by a few hours later, "there was blood on the ground," and the gang members were gone.

Burrell Estelle Carroll was a teacher and principal in area schools. Known most of his life as B. Carroll, he was elected Tarrant County superintendent of public instruction, and in 1919, his name would be carved into the cornerstone of Carroll School. Carroll served as superintendent until 1926. He died in 1938 and is buried in Mount Olivet Cemetery in Fort Worth. (Courtesy of Mary Ann King.)

The Carroll School District No. 99 cornerstone is embedded in the west-side wall of the Carroll School, located north of Highway 114 at the corner of Carroll Avenue and Highland Street. (Author's photograph.)

Carroll School, pictured here in the 1920s, was built by a local contractor, Frank Estill. The Estills built other schools in the area, including Pleasant Run School in Colleyville and Old Bedford School in Bedford; unlike those, Carroll School was one story with no ornamentation. It was "as plain, sturdy, and practical as the farmers who built it," explained Mary Ann King, Carroll's granddaughter. (Courtesy of the Shivers family.)

Families were large, so it wasn't unusual to have three or four children in Carroll School in the same year, as evidenced by these names written on the back of a picture of Carroll students. Teachers were often former students and possibly just a year or two older than some of the students. (Courtesy of the Shivers family.)

Estha McPherson Rodgers attended the Carroll School and remembered, "On the first day of school every year, all the kids brought hoes or tools of some sort, and we chopped up all the weeds and grass burrs and cleaned up the school grounds. I had two younger brothers in school with me, and our mother sent our lunch in one of those old gallon syrup buckets." Rodgers is the first girl pictured on the left in the second row. (Courtesy of the Shivers family.)

The school year began in September—which day depended on when the cotton crop needed picking. Many students from nearby communities were meeting each other for the first time. "We really didn't know each other too well 'til we started school at Carroll," Alno Bailey Shivers remembered. But for her (in the second row, ninth from the left), it was love at first sight when she saw Claude Shivers (first row, fifth from the left). (Courtesy of the Shivers family.)

In 1871, the Texas Board of Education mandated that girls devote two days a week to needlework. By the time Carroll School opened, needlework was long gone from the curriculum, and extracurricular activities were available for girls. "I played on the ball team for about five years," Alno Bailey Shivers recalled. "And I could have gone on further to play, but my dad wouldn't permit me to go." (Courtesy of the Shivers family.)

By the late 1920s, many families saw their children move off the farm and into nearby cities for better-paying jobs. Claude Shivers's older brother, Cloyce Shivers (second row, on the left), was 16 when he played ball on the boys basketball team. After he graduated 10th grade, he married and headed to the big city, Fort Worth. (Courtesy of the Shivers family.)

Before 1921, Texas teachers needed only to pass an examination to be certified. Fannie Lou Throop grew up in Grapevine, and when she was 19, she taught school in Denton County—about the same time as this picture of Carroll students was taken. "I had a teacher's certificate that I had gotten through summer school," Throop recalled. "My qualifications were not very high, but they were not required then like they are now, of course." (Courtesy of the Shivers family.)

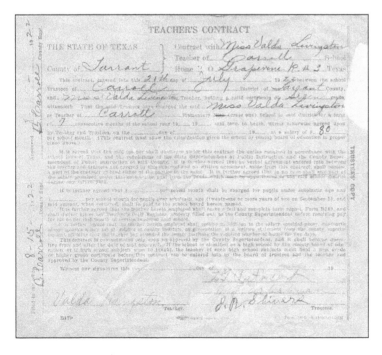

Teacher pay varied from county to county. Fannie Lou Throop remembered earning $70 a month. "We didn't know but what we were getting rich," she said. Valda Livingston's contract with Carroll School shows she made more; she was also required to turn in her "teacher's daily register, properly filled out" before receiving her pay. Notice the signatures of Supt. B. Carroll and J. R. Shivers, one of the school's original trustees. (Courtesy of the Shivers family.)

74

On the back of this picture, Alno Bailey wrote, "Last year at school." Graduating from the 10th grade was bittersweet for her. She wanted to stay in school but was needed at home to help take care of her stepbrother, who suffered from polio and to whom she was very close. A few years later, Bailey married her sweetheart, Claude Shivers, and the couple followed Cloyce Shivers, Claude's brother, to Fort Worth to live. Bailey is standing in the second row, third girl from the left. (Courtesy of the Shivers family.)

John Dolford "Bob" Jones, shown here in an undated photograph, was born in 1850 near Little Rock, Arkansas, to Leazer Jones, a white businessman who raised racehorses, and his slave girl, Lizzie. Leazer and Lizzie had four other children, and around 1859, the family moved to Texas and bought a farm between Roanoke and present-day Southlake. Bob worked for his father herding sheep and cattle until the end of the War Between the States, when he was set free. (Courtesy of the Jones family.)

When Bob Jones was about 11, his father returned to Arkansas, where he had left a white wife and children. Bob and his brother, who stayed in Texas with their mother and sisters, would later buy the 60-acre home place from their father. Leazer Jones, pictured here, stayed in touch with his Texas family, and descendants still do. (Courtesy of the Jones family.)

Bob Jones and the woman he married, Almeada "Meady" Chisum, both had prominent white fathers and black mothers who were slaves. Chisum's father was cattle rancher John Simpson Chisum, shown here, and her mother's name was Jensie. When Chisum moved west, he took Jensie and their two daughters to Bonham, bought them a house, and left money to care for the girls. He reportedly visited several times. (Courtesy of the Jones family.)

Bob and Almeada, shown here in her later years, met in Bonham at a dance. He visited her several times and asked her to come to his farm to visit. According to an interview she gave in 1941, Almeada told Bob "if he would bring his sister in a two-horse wagon, she would go back with them for a visit. So the next trip he came in a covered wagon and brought his sister, Georgia Ann, so Meady returned with them to make the family a visit. Bob took her to Dallas to take the train for the return trip home. When Bob made the third trip, they were married at her sister Harriet's home. They loaded her possessions in a covered wagon and came to their home [in present-day Southlake] where they had 10 children." (Courtesy of the Jones family.)

This picture of the Jones family was taken around 1900 at their home. The house sat on a hill near White Chapel Boulevard at the north end of present-day Bob Jones Park. From left to right are (first row) Bob Jones (holding Jinks), Artie, Hattie, Emma, and Almeada (holding Emory); (second row) Eugie, June, Virgie, Alice, and Jim. (Courtesy of the Charles H. Young family.)

The Bob Jones home began as a log cabin covered with boards. As the family grew, so did the house. When completed, it had two stories, a main room with a large fireplace, four or five bedrooms, a dining room, a kitchen, a balcony, and porches all around. (Courtesy of the Jones family.)

The ornate trim on the balcony of the Joneses' house, one of the grandest in the area, would have required the use of a jigsaw. Manufactured stock trims that could be ordered from a catalog and shipped by railroad were also available. The roof would have been finished with wood shingles. (Courtesy of the Jones family.)

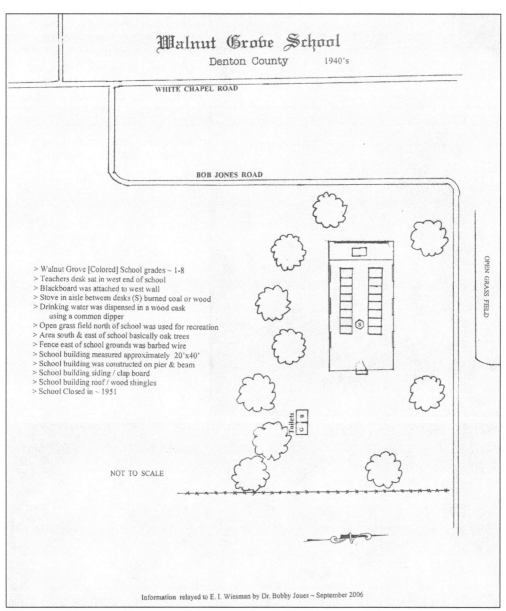

Walnut Grobe School

Denton County   1940's

WHITE CHAPEL ROAD

BOB JONES ROAD

> Walnut Grove [Colored] School grades ~ 1-8
> Teachers desk sat in west end of school
> Blackboard was attached to west wall
> Stove in aisle between desks (S) burned coal or wood
> Drinking water was dispensed in a wood cask
>   using a common dipper
> Open grass field north of school was used for recreation
> Area south & east of school basically oak trees
> Fence east of school grounds was barbed wire
> School building measured approximately 20'x40'
> School building was constructed on pier & beam
> School building siding / clap board
> School building roof / wood shingles
> School Closed in ~ 1951

OPEN GRASS FIELD

Toilets G B

NOT TO SCALE

Information relayed to E. I. Wiesman by Dr. Bobby Jones ~ September 2006

The Jones children could not attend the area's white public schools, so Bob Jones built a one-room school next to his house and named it Walnut Grove. "The only pupils attending were my cousins and one other Negro family who had moved into the area to work," granddaughter Betty Jones Foreman recalled. "There were other children enrolled, but they had to help gather the crops and didn't usually begin school until October, but my education was important to my parents, and they encouraged going to school." This drawing, by local historian E. I. Wiesman, shows what the school looked like, as remembered by Dr. Bobby Jones, Bob Jones's grandson. Of note is the rerouting of Bob Jones Road, which now runs due east from White Chapel Boulevard; the spot where the school once sat is now a residential area. (Courtesy of E. I. Wiesman.)

The Jones family farmed, but the family business was cattle. The boys learned early how to raise and trade cows, horses, and hogs—including prize Poland China hogs, which they showed in stock show competitions. From left to right are Jim, Jinks, and Emory. June is seated. (Courtesy of Marie Grigsby.)

The girls learned to cook, do household chores, milk the cows, and tend the garden. From left to right are (first row) Artie and Virgie; (second row) Hattie, Alice, Eugie, and Emma. (Courtesy of Marie Grigsby.)

The note set on the Jones family Bible shares "our favorite verses" from the scriptures including Matthew 5:6: "Blessed are they that do hunger and thirst after righteousness, for they shall be filled;" Matthew 5:4: "Blessed are they that mourn, for they shall be comforted;" and Philippians 4:11: "Not that I speak in respect of want, for I have learned in whatever state I am, therewith to be content." The Jones family and other African Americans attended Mount Carmel Baptist Church, which sat near Walnut Grove School and drew attendees well into the 1940s. (Courtesy of Marie Grigsby.)

Bob Jones, seen here with his grandson Emory Odell Jones, was respected for his business acumen as well as his compassion for those in need. Friends tell of his loaning money to neighbors when help was needed. (Courtesy of the Jones family.)

When brothers Emory and Jinks Jones were boys, their grandfather gave them a miniature farm wagon harnessed to a nanny goat. From then on, according to Jinks's wife, Lula Williams Jones, "they were partners through life." The brothers showed their prized hogs together and "won several Grand Championships over the forty years they competed in the various shows," she recalled. (Courtesy of the Charles H. Young family.)

Wealthy Negro's Funeral Attended by White Friends

ROANOKE, Dec. 28.—As many white people as colored gathered in the Baptist church here Sunday to pay final tribute to Bob Jones, 86-year-old negro citizen and wealthy landowner.

The crowd of 500 which jammed the white people's church was said to be the largest funeral gathering ever witnessed in the community and the occasion itself unprecedented. Many came from out-of-town.

A negro preacher from Pilot Point had charge of the services, but the white host pastor, Rev. T. Lynn Stewart, assisted.

Elaborate floral offerings banked the casket. Burial was in a plot of the Medlin Cemetery set aside for Jones when the burial ground was established by the white owner, the late J. W. Medlin.

Bob Jones, whose full name was John Dolphin Jones, founded the Jones negro settlement near Roanoke in 1870 several years after he came to Texas from a plantation near Fort Smith, Ark. He bought his first 60 acres of land from his father and at his death his property holdings amounted to about 1,000 acres, including the large two-story house in which he lived.

Bob Jones died in 1936 and was eulogized by local writer and historian Mary Daggett Lake. "The world has all too few men of the caliber of Bob Jones," Lake wrote. "And there is need for them today. They built a structure, a foundation, in this State that is substantial, strong, and secure. My father and Bob Jones used to ride here together—trail-driver mates they were—and often, I imagine, at night they bedded down together under the stars to await the coming of the dawn when they should round up the cattle and travel on. And who knows but that today, they may be traveling together across the level prairies of Eternity." Notice the incorrect spelling of Jones's middle name, which was Dolford. (Courtesy of R. E. Smith.)

Leazer Jones and his wife, Mary, had eight children, some of whom are seen here along with other descendants in the 1940s. Capt. Jink Jones was the youngest, born in 1872, and lived until age 90. When he traveled to the area, he visited the Bob Jones family members to pay his respects. (Captain Jink did not have an "s" in his name, though his nephew Jinks did.) (Courtesy of the Jones family.)

Claude Shivers, seen here, showed his hogs in livestock shows. Such competitions as well as youth clubs, including the Jack County Boys' Corn Club, the Fort Worth Stockyards Pig Clubs, and home demonstration clubs for girls, were offered by county extension services as early as 1914. (Courtesy of the Shivers family.)

Almost everyone went to church often. "You'd go to church and Sunday school and then prayer meeting," explained Lizzie Higgins, whose father, William Day, was a longtime preacher at Lonesome Dove Baptist Church. And then there were baptisms in the branch, the small creek that ran north across Dove Road toward Lonesome Dove church. Claude Shivers is the last boy on the left. (Courtesy of the Shivers family.)

Everyone had or knew someone who had a Brownie camera. It was preloaded with film and cost $25. After the owner took up to 100 pictures, she mailed the camera to the Eastman-Kodak Company in Rochester, New York. Prints and a fully reloaded camera were returned to the owner, all for $10. This picture is of members of the L. N. Bailey family on their farm in the White's Chapel community. (Courtesy of the Shivers family.)

Pictures like this one of the L. N. Bailey family might have ended up on a postcard, a popular way of staying in touch. In 1908, when the population of the United States was about 89 million, more than 600 million picture postcards were mailed. (Courtesy of the Shivers family.)

Sisters Alno (left) and Eunice Bailey (right), along with other family members, are pictured in front of the "old house," as Alno described it on the back of the photograph. Between 1880 and 1930, eighteen million acres of the piney woods timber in East Texas were cut and used to build homes and businesses. The old Bailey house was likely built of wood cut from this first growth of East Texas pine. By the late 1920s, there were several newer houses on the 200-acre Bailey property, which had been pieced together over decades, beginning with a log cabin that was built on the land in the 1870s. (Courtesy of the Shivers family.)

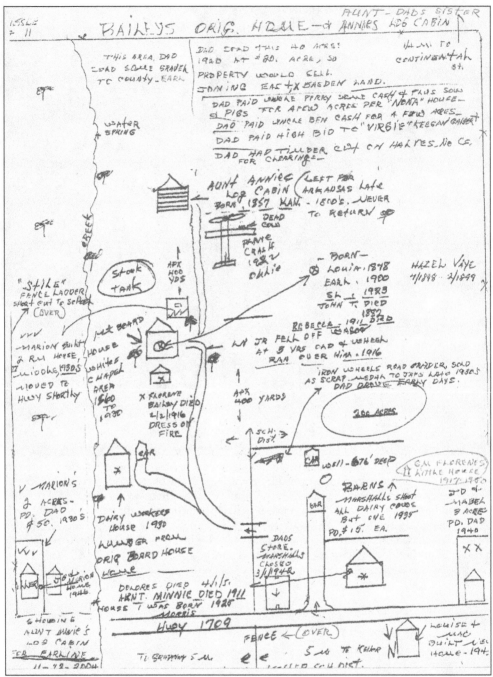

This map of the Bailey property, drawn by descendant Morris Bailey, is a charming picture of one family's history, beginning with Aunt Annie's log cabin and the notation, "Left for Arkansas late 1800s. Never to return." Notice the fence line at the bottom of the drawing with two arrows pointing in opposite directions: "To Grapevine 5 M," and "5 M to Keller." According to Morris Bailey, as late as 2007, the fence was still there. On the left side of the map is a stile, or fence ladder. All the Bailey brothers and sisters "walked to White's Chapel School over this ladder stile," Bailey explained in his notes. (Courtesy of the Shivers family.)

On the farm as elsewhere, people were proud of their cars and trucks. Claude Shivers was no exception. The unidentified person in the window looks like he's having fun. (Courtesy of the Shivers family.)

Sisters Alno (left) and Eunice Bailey (right) stand in front of the family's automobile in the late 1920s. Alno wrote on the back of this picture, "I made my dress." (Courtesy of the Shivers family.)

The popularity of motorized vehicles soon brought attention to the condition of roads, most of which were dirt. In 1930, fewer than 10,000 miles of Texas roads were paved, but by the end of the decade, WPA workers had paved and improved over 21,000 miles of road. Local clubs and organizations were encouraged to clean up the roads in their area, and many donated supplies and labor to build roadside parks. State highway beautification programs were begun and, in 1933, the Office of Landscape Architect was created to modify the roads for automobile travelers driving to Dallas to celebrate the Texas Centennial. Claude Shivers and his passengers, seen here, are ready to hit the road. (Courtesy of the Shivers family.)

By the 1930s, the oil and gas business across the state offered new jobs to farmers and their sons. One such enterprise was the filling station. L. N. Bailey is pictured here in front of his service station and grocery store. As his daughter Alno Bailey Shivers recalled, "If someone needed groceries, he'd let them have them, and if he got the money, OK, and if he didn't, OK. . . . We wasn't rich, but we had a fair living." The station and grocery store faced FM 1709. (Courtesy of the Shivers family.)

Dressed in their Sunday best are Alno (second from left), Eunice (third from left), and L. N. Bailey (right). Mettie Bailey, L. N.'s second wife, is at far left in what appears be the family's summer kitchen or an outbuilding for their dairy business. Notice the milk can and pans hanging next to Mettie. (Courtesy of the Shivers family.)

The wedding picture of Carroll School sweethearts Alno and Claude Shivers was taken in 1927. (Courtesy of the Shivers family.)

The well-dressed Alno, who by then was living in Fort Worth, returned to the "old home place" for a visit. (Courtesy of the Shivers family.)

The number of stories about Bonnie and Clyde could fill a bank building. In 1934, they gunned down officers H. D. Murphy, left, and E. B. Wheeler, below, on Dove Road east of Highway 114. Some say other members of the Barrow gang did the shootings, but one local doubted it because, as he said, "it happened just like they did things. They'd shoot you, and ask questions later." (Courtesy of the Texas Department of Public Safety.)

Five

A RICH PAST,
A PROSPEROUS FUTURE
1935–1970

The Depression was hard on the nation, but in what is now Southlake, people already were used to not having much. Because they raised their own food, no one went hungry, and work, church, and homemade fun filled their time.

Highway 114, completed in the 1930s, was a boon to the area. During World War II, young men again left to serve their country. Afterward, as happened all over the United States, many migrated to cities. For the first time in the state's history, more Texans lived in cities than in the country.

In 1945, the U.S. government authorized the building of a lake that would tame Denton Creek and supply water primarily to Dallas-area cities. Soon the government began buying up, then condemning, land needed for the lake—some 12,000 acres—much of which it purchased for about $55 an acre. "Dairy farms and truck or produce farms were where the lake is now," recalled resident Mabel Cate. Some people were angry and suspicious of the process. "It was a sad time because they had no choice." The Army Corps of Engineers completed Lake Grapevine in 1952.

People living here in the 1950s say they would have been content to stay rural, free of city taxes and controls. If Hurst hadn't begun an effort to annex several unincorporated areas, there wouldn't have been a rush in the summer of 1956 to incorporate. A petition was circulated, and when the vote was taken, 30 people had voted for incorporation and 24 against. Colleyville and Westlake also incorporated in 1956. The lake and the chance to live on acreage lured many newcomers, but the names of longtime families could still be heard in and around Southlake.

As the area prospered, city services were added, and the schools grew. The Dragons football team won their first district championship in 1965, the same year that something big landed on Southlake's doorstep—an international airport. Since it opened in 1974, the Dallas–Fort Worth International Airport has brought people and prosperity to Southlake and its neighboring communities.

When the stock market crashed in October 1929, Texas's economy was humming, which helped lessen—at least for a while—the fear of a failing economy. Farmers, accustomed to the ups and downs of crop prices, made do. Young mothers, like Hazel Pearl Neal Tate, who grew up farming the Grapevine Prairie, worked hard for their families. Tate, seen in this 1935 photograph, is holding her daughter Laura Mae; daughter Merrill Dean faces the camera. (Courtesy of the Stacy family.)

Farmers shipped their milk by rail, or, closer to home, some drove "milk routes" delivering fresh milk and butter to town dwellers. Dairy farmer Frank Neal milks a cow on the family farm on the Grapevine Prairie in this 1940s photograph. (Courtesy of the Stacy family.)

Many dairymen lived and worked in the Denton Creek bottomlands north of present-day Southlake. Standing in front of Arthur and Dolah Tate and their four sons are two longtime Southlake residents—former Southlake mayor John R. Tate on the left, and his cousin, Merrill Tate Stacy, mother of another former mayor, Rick Stacy, on the right. (Courtesy of the Stacy family.)

Carroll School added a 10th grade in the 1930s and continued to educate the young people of the community, as seen in this 1936 photograph. But for years, people in neighboring communities considered Carroll a country school that didn't measure up and called it "Chigger Hill," which, for many, were fighting words. (Southlake Historical Society collection.)

Young men headed off to fight in World War II, and the pace of life quickened when soldiers, home on leave, wanted to reconnect with friends and had only a short time to do it. Courtships kindled quickly. One such romance began in 1945, when "Johnny" Tate, stationed in the Pacific, was home on a short stay and dated Kathryn McPherson. Tate, shown here, was discharged the following June, and by October, the couple was married. (Courtesy of John R. Tate.)

The war required manpower, and so did farming. Bill McPherson and his wife, Eula, bought 300 acres west of Roanoke in 1932. With the help of their 10 children, they farmed and raised dairy cows. But as the boys left to marry or join the service, McPherson couldn't manage by himself. In 1945, he sold his farm to retire to "his small sandy-land farm," wrote his daughter, Kathryn McPherson Tate, seen here on the porch of their Southlake home on Dove Road. (Courtesy of John R. Tate.)

Board's Store was a gathering place located on Continental Boulevard at Brumlow Avenue. "It was like a 7-Eleven," Wanda Stowe recalls, "but smaller." Stowe remembers summer visits in the 1940s with her aunt and uncle, Etta and Owen Brumlow, for whom Brumlow Avenue is named. For fun, she rode horses with the Chasteen girls, who lived about a mile away. "They would come from their house to Board's Store," she explained. "And we'd ride wherever we wanted to." Seen here in the 1940s are, from left to right, Beulah Board, Azzie Hardin, Nannie Webb, and Eula Blevins. (Courtesy of R. E. Smith.)

There is a small tombstone in front of the baskets of tomatoes in this 1940s photograph. This is Easter Cemetery, located on the north side of FM 1709 near Gateway Drive and named for early settler Thomas Easter. At one time, the cemetery held as many as 11 sandstone grave markers. Later landowners built a hog pen (the boards along the left) beneath the trees, and over time, the hogs uprooted some of the markers. Larry Banks grew up on 64 acres south of the cemetery. He and his brother, Darrell, earned 10¢ for each basket of tomatoes they picked for the Davis family, the owners of the property that included the cemetery. From left to right are Darrell Banks, Lillian Davis, Donald Shockey, and Jim Davis. (Southlake Historical Society collection.)

The Pleasant Hill Advent Christian Church stood across FM 1709 from the White's Chapel Cemetery for more than 60 years. Even if devoted members had moved away, they would drive back to Pleasant Hill for church on Sunday and wouldn't miss the annual Mother's Day basket dinner. The church was built by its members in 1937. (Courtesy of Shivers family.)

If you grew up in the Pleasant Hill Advent Christian Church, you most likely were "converted" in the tabernacle, also known as the arbor. Older members recall church dinners when women cooked over an open fire and brought homemade cakes and pies. "That was really living," one member said. "We may have had to take paper fans and fan [ourselves], but we had a good time." (Courtesy of Shivers family.)

The Texas Conference of Advent Christian Churches built a conference center behind the church in 1937 that included a dormitory, kitchen, and dining hall. The last week of July, Adventist churches from across the state would send their members to Pleasant Hill for their annual conference. (Courtesy of John R. Tate.)

Rebecca Shivers Utley grew up attending the annual youth "encampments"—summer camps—and remembers staying in the dorms cooled by "swamp coolers." Activities for the teenagers, such as the several seen in this photograph, included swimming and a midweek trip to Six Flags theme park. "Remember, we were camping out in the middle of July, with the benefit of only a few fans," Utley said. "And we were still expected to iron our dresses or blouses and wear hose each evening." (Courtesy of the Stacy family.)

The razing of the Pleasant Hill church in the 1990s was mourned by many, including members of other congregations. "I have a friend that went to another church and she said, 'Even though I didn't go there, that church was part of me,' " one member recalled. (Courtesy of Shivers family.)

"Many were the members who went into the baptismal waters with Brother Day," one old-timer recalled. William Day moved to Texas from Tennessee in 1911 "because he was called to preaching," explained his daughter, Lizzie Day Higgins. "And he thought if he left Tennessee, he wouldn't have to answer that call. But he answered the call after he got here." In 1948, Brother Day (in suspenders) was still baptizing believers. (Courtesy of the Joyce family.)

During his 25-year tenure at Lonesome Dove Baptist Church, Brother Day performed weddings and funerals (some for the early pioneers who settled the area) and was included in many other family celebrations. He is shown here, in the middle of the picture dressed in a suit and wearing glasses, celebrating with Joyce family members at a church gathering in the 1940s. (Courtesy of the Joyce family.)

Carroll School started with 9 grades, then added a 10th. Later it dropped to 8 grades, and students attended grades 9 through 12 in Grapevine. During World War II, several Carroll students recall leaving class to wave flags for the soldiers in the troop convoys that traveled along Highway 114. (Courtesy of the Stacy family.)

When work began to build Lake Grapevine in 1947, residents remember it as a sad time. Mable Cate recalled, "We had relatives and friends that'd lived [on the Denton Creek land] all their life. And when those houses started coming out—they moved a lot of them to Grapevine—it wasn't funny. But they told us it was progress, and 'you've got to go with progress.' So we did." (Courtesy of the U.S. Army Corps of Engineers.)

Locals would drive into the bottomlands to visit the site. "We'd go down there every Sunday. That was a big deal for us, watching them take dirt out for the dam," remembered Darrell Shockey, who grew up between Roanoke and Southlake. Wanda Stowe and her husband, Bill, drove down to the site in their first automobile and had their picture taken. Notice the cars driving along the dam road in the background. (Courtesy of Wanda Stowe.)

Once the dam was built, the question was how long it would take to fill up. "And it was kind of amusing that engineers worked and worked, trying to figure out how long it'd take that lake to fill up," Mabel Cate remembered. "We knew it depended on the rainfall, and it could be fast. So they came up with a figure of 10 years. It started raining. And it filled up in a week." (Courtesy of the Tarrant County College District Archives, Fort Worth, Texas.)

Among the families displaced by the construction of Lake Grapevine were descendants of Bob Jones. They all moved, except for Eugie Jones Thomas, Jones's daughter. "I fought them [Army Corps of Engineers] . . . it went to Washington. Then one day the mailman brought me a letter. 'You can keep all of your property,' it said. My home was more to me than money," Thomas stated. (Courtesy of the U.S. Army Corps of Engineers.)

The Grapevine Auction Barn and Jones Café weren't even located in Grapevine but rather at the southeast corner of Highway 114 and White Chapel Boulevard. Brothers Jinks and Emory Jones partnered up in 1948 to open a business. "We had handled [cattle] all our lives, so we got thinking we could open up a place to handle them," Jinks Jones said. This photograph of Jinks Jones was taken in 1977. (Courtesy of the Jones family.)

The cattle auction business soon included horses. Zena Rucker and her husband, Bill, moved to the area in 1960 and attended many auctions. "On one day of the week they auctioned cattle. The place would be packed to the top of the bleachers," Zena Rucker said. "Then there would be a separate day for horses. Horsemen from far and wide would start arriving sometimes the night before. It was really exciting." (Courtesy of the Jones family.)

The Jones brothers, partners since childhood, married sisters Lula (left) and Elnora Williams (right). The sisters ran the Jones Café, which is believed to be the first integrated café in Texas. The food was simple—chili, hamburgers, homemade pies—and good. The café was small, remembers Betty Jones Foreman, Jinks and Lula's only child. "Maybe 20-by-20, as I recall," Foreman said, "with one eating area." (Courtesy of the Jones family.)

"Mama and Aunt Lula didn't open an integrated café. They opened a café," explained Bobby Jones, Emory and Elnora's son. "Black truck drivers would stop on the road, and they would come in the back door and ask if they could have a soda or a sandwich," Betty Jones Foreman explained. "My mother told them, 'I'll serve you if you come in the front door . . . this is a family business and I'll serve who I want.' " Seen here standing outside of the Jones Café in the early 1980s are Bob Jones's grandsons Bill (left) and Bobby (right) as well as Bobby's stepdaughter, Donna Pockrus. (Courtesy of the Jones family.)

The partnership between the Jones brothers ended with Emory's death in 1968. Elnora died in 1972. Lula continued to run the sisters' flea market, started in the 1940s and held in the auction barn, until her death in 1980. Jinks died in 1981. The property was sold to the Stacy family, which continued the flea market until 2007. This picture, taken on Eugie Jones Thomas's property in the 1970s, shows Jinks, his wife, Lula, and his daughter, Betty Jones Foreman. (Courtesy of Betty Jones Foreman.)

The Jones family was also known for its annual community-wide picnic, held by Bob Jones on his farm in the fall after harvest time. Jinks and Emory continued the event at the auction barn until the 1970s. There were children's games, adult baseball games, and food. People brought their musical instruments and played while others danced. Old-timers still talk about the Jones family picnics. (Courtesy of Betty Jones Foreman.)

"Yes It's Picnic Time Again"

Jones Brothers
August **ANNUAL PICNIC**
13, 14, 15 - 1964
Thurs. Fri. Sat.

5 miles west of Grapevine on Hiway 114
at the Grapevine Auction Barn

WALTER JETTON'S
BARBQ SERVICE
will furnish Bar-B-Q & their famous
Fried Pies
Plenty of Cold Drinks

WILLIAM A SCHAFER'S SCIENCE FAIR
EXPOSITION. WILL FUNISH ENTERTAINMENT
FOR THE MIDWAY.
Jinks & Emory Jones committee on arrangements

Families wanted a piece of the American Dream. By 1950, Texas was more urban than rural, although farming remained key to the state's prosperity. Merrill Tate Stacy, seen here with her husband, R. J., had grown up on the Grapevine Prairie and in the area west of Grapevine. After the couple married, they moved to Dallas, then back to Grapevine, where they raised three boys. The couple settled in Southlake in the 1970s. (Courtesy of the Stacy family.)

One summer evening in the 1950s, Bruce McCombs, then 16 or 17, got the urge to drive the family car to Keller on the Keller-Grapevine Road—now known as Southlake Boulevard. "I drove to Keller and back," he recalled, "and did not see *one* car." A few years later, traffic had picked up, as this photograph of the intersection of FM 1709 and Davis Boulevard shows. (Courtesy of the City of Southlake.)

As in all small towns, everyone knew everyone. "It was a neat place to raise the kids," recalled Marilyn Tucker, who grew up in the Minter's Chapel community on the Grapevine Prairie. "They had the same advantage as I did . . . to grow up in a small area where you got caught no matter what you did, by a parent." Seen here with their bikes are the sons of Johnny and Kathryn Tate, Robert Anthony Tate (left) and John Michael Tate (right), at the family home on White Chapel Boulevard. (Courtesy of John R. Tate.)

New folks moving here just wanted a little land. Others, like the Joyce family, had a long history in the area. Here Versie Ola Foster Joyce and Cloyce Patrick Joyce are celebrating their son Fred's college graduation. The area west of Grapevine was growing and about to make a name for itself. (Courtesy of the Joyce family.)

If Southlake had to pick a father, it might be Clovis Monroe Gordon—C. M. to his family. Barbara Gordon recalls in August 1956, when her husband came home with important news: Hurst was working to annex unincorporated areas, including theirs. The Gordons phoned neighbors, and within days a petition was signed asking for an election to incorporate a new town. (Courtesy of the Gordon family.)

"All of us live here because we like it," wrote the drafters of the proposed incorporation. A group hand-carried the required paperwork to Austin. Notices of an election were ordered posted in three public places, one of which was Carroll School. On September 22, the vote was taken—30 for, 24 against. On September 25, 1956, the town of Southlake was born. (Courtesy of the Gordon family.)

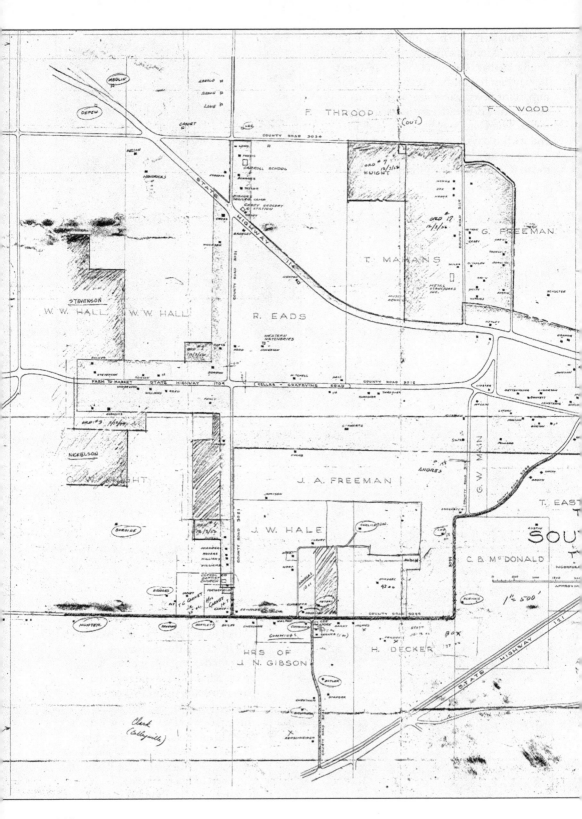

"I am the kid who came up with the name Southlake," Suzanne Eubanks Louth told the historical society. "I suggested it needed to be a 'geography name' that tells where we are on a map. . . . I was very proud when my dad [A. Gail Eubanks] later showed me the final papers that showed Southlake 'on a map.'" Here is the original map of incorporated Southlake. (Courtesy of the Gordon family.)

Southlake measured 1.62 square miles when it began. This view of FM 1709 and White Chapel Boulevard was taken in the 1960s, and it shows how undeveloped the town was. White's Chapel United Methodist Church is seen to the right of the intersection, near a grove of trees. (Courtesy of White's Chapel United Methodist Church.)

When Southlake incorporated, large tracts of land remained undisturbed. This pastoral property belonged to a member of the McPherson family as early as 1895. The Fechtel family bought it in 1950 and built a chicken hatchery. In 1996, the land was purchased for the site of Southlake Town Square. After attempts by concerned citizens to move it, the 1919 farmhouse was burned by the fire department as a training exercise. (Courtesy of Aloha Payne.)

It was common to see long gravel driveways leading into farms and ranchettes scattered around town. Property owners outside the original 1.62 square miles requested to be annexed into the town. Their property had to be "adjacent and contiguous to the Town of Southlake." The first property owners to receive annexation approval were Mayor A. Gail Eubanks and his wife, June. (Courtesy of Aloha Payne.)

By March 1957, 12 square miles of owner-requested annexations were approved. The town's first zoning ordinance, establishing the length of a city block and the width of major streets, was approved. With an eye toward future needs, the mayor suggested the aldermen join him in paying friendly calls on the county commissioners in charge of roads "to establish friendly relations before we need to ask favors of them." The driveway shown here wound its way from the C. M. Gordon home to Southlake Boulevard. (Courtesy of Ann Gordon Swindell.)

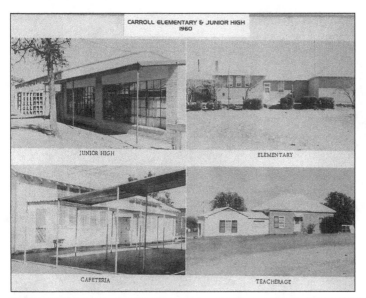

CARROLL ELEMENTARY & JUNIOR HIGH
1960

JUNIOR HIGH   ELEMENTARY

CAFETERIA   TEACHERAGE

One Saturday a month, the town council met at Carroll School. In 1959, voters upgraded the school system to an independent school district, and principal Jack D. Johnson was named superintendent, a job he held for 30 years. When Johnson and his wife, Modean, moved to Southlake in 1957, the school had eight grades, 125 students, three teachers, and a three-member board of trustees. (Southlake Historical Society collection.)

Carroll Elementary & Junior High
1960
(9ᵗʰ Grade)
First Football Team At Carroll School

SWEETHEART: Carolyn Ragsdale. COACH: H. G. Griffin. Top Row: Billy Roe, Mike Vester, Jimmy Graham, Buddie Venable, Anthony Tate, Larry Lee, Douglas Crumbaker, Philip Vester, Danny Rodgers, Tommy Schell, James Crawford. Bottom Row: Eddie Cheatham, Steven Carney, Jimmy Guess, Douglas Depew, Roy Millican, Jack Roe, Ted McPherson, Mike Sanders, Leon Drosihn, Charles Kelsch.

Dragon football began in 1960. Superintendent Johnson actually began the school's athletic program with basketball. But it would be the football team that brought Carroll recognition on a state and national level. And Johnson recalled that although there was little money to start the football program, community volunteers worked together to make it happen. (Southlake Historical Society collection.)

120

In 1964, Lavon Baird became the town's first postmistress. Mailboxes were built inside the former Torian service station at the corner of Carroll Avenue and Highway 114. Baird is seen in the window on the right. Her friend Mollie Cummings in is the window to the left, which led to Baird's adjacent antique store. The man with his back to the camera is Mayor Paul Schell, who served from 1964 to 1967. (Southlake Historical Society collection.)

After Southlake's first chief of police was appointed, Carroll Independent School District administrators appeared before the town council to urge them to allow Chief Keller Austin to hire additional officers immediately—help was needed to better police all upcoming football games. Administrators offered to pay for the officers' shirts and pants. The council approved their request and threw in the money for jackets and badges to complete the uniforms The city's first police force included, from left to right, Chief Austin next to Mayor Schell, officer Lloyd Brown, and officer James Davis. (Courtesy of the City of Southlake.)

In 1966, the first volunteer fire department was formed. The chief was Howard Moffat, seen here. A Tarrant County fire marshal invited to speak to the new group mandated that the members become a "bona fide organization" before they could receive county funds. So plans were made to meet the first Thursday of each month and to provide two training sessions a month to the approximately 25 volunteers. (Courtesy of the City of Southlake.)

In April 1969, R. P. "Bob" Steele was hired as fire chief, and he served the city for 25 years. Steele and his wife, Crystal, were well-known behind the counter at Casey's Grocery in Southlake. Long before Steele was named fire chief, Casey's served as an early city hall in exchange for a monthly rent of $5. When Southlake purchased its first fire truck, it was parked outside Casey's Grocery. (Courtesy of the Steele family.)

In 1964, the Civil Aeronautics Board ordered Dallas and Fort Worth to come up with an agreed-upon location for a joint airport. Finally, in December 1968, the two cities reached an agreement, and ground was broken for the Dallas–Fort Worth Regional Airport at the intersection of Euless, Irving, Coppell, and Grapevine. Work got underway in January 1969. (Courtesy of the Dallas–Fort Worth International Airport.)

In an ironic twist, some people had moved their houses from the Denton Creek bottomlands in the 1940s to the Grapevine Prairie, only to be displaced again in the 1960s by the construction of Dallas–Fort Worth Airport. (Courtesy of the Dallas–Fort Worth International Airport.)

Seventeen thousand acres were purchased to build the airport. It's taking shape here. (Courtesy of the Dallas–Fort Worth International Airport.)

The land cost $68 million. Dallas–Fort Worth Airport would ultimately cover more than 29.8 square miles. (Courtesy of the Dallas–Fort Worth International Airport.)

This plesiosaur, dated at 70 million years old, was excavated during the early earthmoving for the Dallas–Fort Worth Airport. The remains of the 25-foot-long creature were restored by graduate students of the Shuler Museum of Paleontology at Southern Methodist University, paid for through a grant from Braniff Airlines in the 1970s. (Courtesy of the Tarrant County College District Archives, Fort Worth, Texas.)

The airport helped Southlake take off and become—according to the U.S. Census Bureau in 2007—the city with the highest median income with a population between 20,000 and 65,000 in the United States. (Courtesy of the Tarrant County College District Archives, Fort Worth, Texas.)

The Southlake water tower is a familiar sight around town. (Courtesy of the City of Southlake.)

The Southlake Historical Society is working to raise awareness and to encourage the reuse and preservation of the 1919 Carroll School. "For more than four decades, Carroll School was the center of life in the close-knit, hard-working community known as the 'area west of Grapevine'—present-day Southlake," wrote SHS president Anita Robeson. Please visit the society's Web site at www.southlakehistory.org. (Author's photograph.)

BIBLIOGRAPHY

Fehrenbach, T. R. *Lone Star: A History of Texas and the Texans*. New York: Tess Press/Black Dog & Leventhal Publishers, Inc., 1968, 2000.

Francaviglia, Richard. *The Cast Iron Forest: A Natural and Cultural History of the Cross Timbers*. Austin: University of Texas Press, 2000.

Greene, A. C. *A Place Called Dallas*. Dallas: Dallas County Heritage Society, Inc., 1975.

Haley, James L. *Texas: From Spindletop through World War II*. New York: St. Martin's Press, 1993.

Historic Preservation Council for Tarrant County, Texas. *Tarrant County Historical Resources Survey: Selected Tarrant County Communities*. Fort Worth: Historic Preservation Council for Tarrant County, Texas, 1990.

Hogue, Frances Higgins. *1913 Heritage Quilt of Lonesome Dove Baptist Church*. Unpublished paper, 1995.

Hoover, Fran W., ed. *The Lonesome Coo of the Dove: The History of Lonesome Dove Baptist Church Founded in 1846*. Unpublished paper, 1996.

O'Donnell, Pearl Foster. *Trek to Texas, 1770–1870*. Fort Worth: Branch-Smith, 1966.

Patterson, Michael, "Civil War Veterans of Northeast Tarrant County," *Tarrant County TxGenWeb*, August 22, 2009, www.rootsweb.ancestry.com (February 29, 2008).

Southlake Journal. "50th Anniversary Southlake." September 15, 2006.

Tate, Sandra K., ed. *Grapevine's Most Unforgettable Characters*. Marceline, MO: Walsworth Publishing Company, 2006.

Texas State Historical Association. *The Handbook of Texas Online*, www.tshaonline.org (February 14, 2008).

The University of Texas College of Liberal Arts. "Aldridge Sawmill." *Texas Beyond History*, www.texasbeyondhistory.net (August 11, 2004).

Wiesman, Elmer I. *An Historical Perspective of Southlake and Its Surroundings*. Self-published, 2006.

Young, Charles H., ed. *Grapevine Area History*. Dallas: Taylor Publishing, 1989.

Visit us at
arcadiapublishing.com